# THE RADOVIĆ RULE

# How to

# Manage
# the Boss

*OR*

THE

# RADOVIĆ RULE

*which says that:*

**(a)**

In any organization, the potential is much greater for the Subordinate to manage his Superior than for the Superior to manage his Subordinate, and

# (b)

The maximum rewards in employment are
not to be found in upward mobility, but
in stability at the rank and file level.

## by Igor Radović

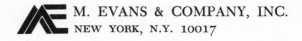 M. EVANS & COMPANY, INC.
NEW YORK, N.Y. 10017

# Illustrations by Stacey Rogers

M. Evans and Company titles are distributed
in the United States by the J. B. Lippincott Company,
East Washington Square, Philadelphia, Pa. 19105
and in Canada by McClelland & Stewart, Ltd., 25
Hollinger Road, Toronto 374, Ontario

To all the executives who so generously
contributed material for this book, and
made royalties from it possible

# Contents

Foreword, 13

A cautionary note, 19

1. On the nature of the subordinate position, 21
2. Selecting the right subordinate position, 29
3. The use of rules and regulations, 39
4. The company one keeps, 49
5. Keeping the Superior insecure and off-balance, 55
6. Tensions, frictions and suspicions among Superiors, 69
7. On giving credit and showing proper respect, 77
8. Information management and the intelligence leak, 89
9. Rumors, 101
10. The woman executive, 109
11. Building a reputation for hard work and competence, 111
12. Individual versus group actions, 121
13. The use of secretarial assistance, 127
14. The underprivileged label, 135
15. The subordinate image, 143
16. Subordinate ethics, 149

Epilogue, 155

# Foreword

Countless books and articles have been written on the Science of Management, and they are without exception, on management of subordinates by Superiors.

The existing professional literature, startling as this may be, contains no studies whatsoever on problems of management of Superiors by subordinates, specifically on the problem of optimization of the performance of the former from the point of view of the latter. This represents a glaring and intolerable void, and is also the cause of a totally unjustified neglect of the great potential of subordinate jobs. Subordinates, after all, by far outnumber Superiors, and in this age of equality and mass enlightenment the rights and interests of the majority must not be given short shrift, not only by the government and the community, at work and at play, but in professional literature as well.

Even to the superficial observer, it is obvious that the nature itself of management is currently undergoing a profound change. Management is rapidly becoming a two-way street, with decisions filtering in increasing numbers from the rank and file to the top executive echelons. This fact also must receive proper recognition which, to date, is altogether lacking in print.

This text is a modest attempt to start filling a gap in the existing body of knowledge on management, and at the same time to provide a much-needed management guide for the benefit of the subordinate, the almost forgotten and unjustly neglected protagonist of organizational life. It also has led, in the course of research associated with it, to the formulation of the Rule printed on the title page of this monograph. In a virtually virgin field of theory and practice of management, where nevertheless a genuine contribution can be made to improve the lot of subordinates—the working masses, no less—a single slim volume such as this one can only scratch the surface. It can only touch upon some basic aspects of management of Superiors by subordinates, and open the door for other, more ambitious groundbreaking studies. It pretends to, and hopes for no more.

This primer concerns itself with both the strategy and the tactics of Management of Superiors by subordinates (or Management of Superiors, for short). It outlines basic principles and gives, mainly for illustrative purposes, concrete examples of their application.

The principles outlined are generally valid, and have no national or ideological boundaries. While every Superior requires a somewhat tailor-made approach, a need for adaptation for individual cases does not go beyond stressing some management principles a little more than others. With proper coaching by a subordinate every Superior becomes the right type of Superior from the subordinate point of view. One Superior, it is true, may need more training than another, as the ability to learn varies from individual to individual.

The methodology developed in this text does not focus on the person of the Superior alone, but considers possibilities for positive change in his working environment as well because, to explain this by a simple analogy, a sinner deprived of his vices is as good as reformed, or better.

The successful application of the Radović Rule does not require any special abilities in a subordinate, only an honest commitment to the subordinate cause. Men of unusually modest mental endowment can achieve unqualified success as subordinates, as in many other walks of life, by consistently following a few simple rules of behavior. Management of Superiors is not an arcane art accessible to a gifted few, but a simple science anyone with diligence can master.

With regret, it must be said that the scope of Management of Superiors is more restricted in small organizations than in the larger ones, and that the principles explained here are only partially applicable in the former. In small organizations the stress is on the work itself, and the human element of a work situation is underplayed and penalized. Fortunately, the day of the large organization, in which the subordinate is given the opportunity to develop his management potential to the full, is with us, and does not appear to be on the wane.

A number of readers might think at first that a book

such as this one will be a divisive influence and will lead to greater conflicts and more strife between Superiors and subordinates, to the detriment of the organization. This is neither the book's intention nor can it be its end result. Quite to the contrary, one of its main objectives is to bring the subordinate into the management process and make him a responsible partner in organizational decision-making. Inevitably, this will give the subordinate a better understanding and appreciation of the Superior's role and functions, and make possible more efficient and harmonious teamwork between the two, to the benefit of the organization. True, the Superior may initially fail to see things this way, but this is only to be expected, because adjustment to something different usually takes time.

It will probably also be said that this guide takes a partisan, subordinate point of view of management problems. This is true, and we have no apologies to offer, as this is how it should be.* And besides, as anybody who has ever been on either side of any issue inevitably finds out sooner or later, those who claim to be objective and impartial are at best brainwashed by the opposition, and at worst openly siding with it.

In the minds of some people, a stigma is attached to the word *subordinate*. It is difficult to understand the reason why. The only place where the subordinate stands below the Superior is on the Organization Chart. Even a cursory analysis will show that in every other relevant aspect—work satisfaction, independence, influence, earning potential, security, professional development, to

---

* Or should, maybe, a trapper's manual be written for the benefit of the bear, the fox and the weasel?

mention only a few of them—the subordinate's position is immeasurably superior to that of the executive. Anybody who, on reflection, still harbors some doubts about this and about the Radović Rule need only read on.*

---

* And we hope this invitation will draw a better response than the travel agency ad for a round trip to Argentina which said: "Invest $699.00 and see the pampas, and if you like them so much the better."

# A cautionary note

This text was written for the genuine subordinate who intends to remain a subordinate and has no desire to be anything else. A false subordinate, who reads this book hoping to find in it advice on how to propel himself into the ranks of Superiors, will be disappointed.

**1**

# On the nature of
# the subordinate position

He that is down need fear no fall. . . .
Paul Bunyan: *Pilgrim's Progress*

The obvious, no offense meant to the reader, is most likely
to be overlooked, and so it is no surprise that some of the
more basic and evident facts about the nature of the subordinate position should need some explaining. One of
these facts is that subordinate jobs truly represent an
uncommon opportunity for the common man of modest
abilities where he can attain complete independence and
achieve total work satisfaction. Another is that this op-

21

portunity exists not only for a select few but, literally speaking, for the broad masses. Yet another is that it can be exploited by following a few simple precepts that this text will describe in some detail. The failure to recognize these basic attributes of subordinate jobs is the principal reason so little advantage is taken of their potential. So that they will be less easily overlooked in the future, we shall now examine them more closely.

## THE SUBORDINATE POSITION
## AND INDEPENDENCE

A subordinate who has identified the largely still unrecognized characteristics of subordinate jobs (such as superficial lack of appeal, indispensability and near-irreplaceability), who knows how to get leverage out of them, and who is determined to remain a subordinate and make the most of it can gain an unmatched degree of independence in relation to his Superior and the system, both in frame of mind and in fact, and can then build his career on top of this.

But let us scrutinize the basis for this independence itself, and see how real and solid it is: The subordinate, the reader will agree, need not keep glancing over his shoulder to make sure nobody will stab him in the back for, being at the bottom of the organizational totem pole, he knows there is no one behind him. A genuine subordinate, for excellent reasons, has no interest whatever in promotion and thus represents no threat to those who, in title, outrank him. In addition, subordinate jobs being unpopular and comparatively easy to find, there is as a rule never any interest on the part of his peers to replace him and, therefore, no need to worry about hostile moves from this direction. *The position of the subordinate is one of great intrinsic security for not only has the subordinate no natural enemies, he is also irreplaceable,* the current attitude among employment seekers toward subordinate jobs being what it is.* There is definitely no need for a man who is irreplaceable to justify his holding his job, to bend docilely to executive whims and fancies, to conform meekly to an organization-sanctioned code of behavior, to compromise with his principles or, out of timidity, to refrain from any actions designed to make his job more to his own liking.

*The strength of the subordinate position,* it cannot be emphasized strongly enough, *is built on independence from, and not dependence on one's Superiors.* The lickspittle approach to professional success and job satisfaction is totally foreign to the science of Management of Superiors, not only on ethical but on pragmatic grounds as well. The Superior's flunky, who stoops to stoop again, is not only deprived of the respect of his colleagues and of the dignity of self-respect, but is also laying the foundation of his carreer on quicksand. He swims and sinks with his patron, and, with current executive turnover showing no signs of abating, he very often sinks and must scramble for a new job or a new sponsor or both. Past experience indicates however, we are happy to add, that the toady who, in some capacity or other, attaches himself to the

---

* This misdirected ambition in vocational goals ("rising" expectations), so prevalent these days among the young, is, incidentally, a striking example of mass aberration, brought about by general literacy and the indiscriminate spreading of education.

persona of a VIP and, like a tickbird, lives off the droppings of the symbiotic partner, is never an authentic
subordinate at heart, but is only a mere executive aspirant
in search of an uncle, a godfather or a good fairy. He is
also, we may add in passing, often characterized by a
complete absence of a brain or identity of his own, having
become purely and simply a mere extension or out-
growth of his master—a "perfect" subordinate, from his
Superior's point of view.

In comparison with the executive aspirant, the real
subordinate fares infinitely better: He does not depend
on his Superior for the fulfillment of his ambitions, for he
already has the job he wants; and he does not have to
worry about keeping his job either, for few positions are
as secure as those that are shunned by job seekers and are
difficult to fill. The real subordinate can have both the
satisfactions and advantages of being his own master and
pay no price for it.


## OPPORTUNITIES FOR INDEPENDENCE

A mounting institutional giantism, possibly a prologue
to extinction, is very much in evidence nowadays in business, government, education, social services and other
places where people make their living; and there is a pervasive and growing interdependence in decision-making
processes everywhere. In these circumstances, *the opportunity of the average individual to achieve independence and success on his own, outside the interlocking
system, is getting close to nil. But he still can achieve
them within the system,* and on his own terms, through

*The subordinate who, like a tick-bird, lives off the droppings of the symbiotic partner, is never an authentic subordinate at heart.*

the nearly unlimited and ever-multiplying job opportunities in the subordinate-employee bracket. His prospects
for this possibility have, in fact, never looked better, and
a quick look at labor statistics, showing that for every
new executive job there are a dozen or more new subordinate jobs, will attest to that fact.

## QUALIFICATIONS REQUIRED

*To become a successful and fulfilled subordinate,
special abilities are not needed. Brilliance is definitely not
required. Mediocrity,* that much maligned and underrated
quality, *can on the contrary be a distinct asset here,* as
long as it is sustained and consistent. For one, it lessens
the dangers of overreaching, a trap that no executive can
resist. It also makes it easier for the subordinate to remain within the boundaries of a simple, tried-and-safe
mode of conduct, and it controls the desire for experi-
mentation that is the undoing of a venturesome imagination. A man of modest abilities can really come into his
own as a subordinate, and leave his mark while perform-
ing within his cerebral means. There is no magic to being
a subordinate success, and besides magic doesn't always
work.* Another qualification not required of the subordinate is to be a "Leader of Men." He therefore need
not try to swagger sillier and bray louder than everybody
else to prove his leadership qualities. Instead, quietly

---

* As, for instance, in the case of the holy man who in his native land
parted the waters when he wanted to cross the rivers, and then came
to New York City and was promptly run over by a cab when he tried
to cross the street against the red light.

and more profitably, he can mind his own business, and leave funny impersonations to those with loftier management aspirations.

## DRAWBACKS AND HAZARDS

It would not serve any useful purpose to delude the reader and maintain that the subordinate position does not have any drawbacks. It does. For instance, because he is a subordinate, an employee will probably have to forego many opportunities, that by comparison are given to the executive in abundance, to learn about the art of compromise, or the virtue of and knack for accommodation, also known sometimes as the spit-and-lick routine.* But then, one should not ask for perfection in anything, other than the flavor of coffee, and the subordinate ought to be prepared to make occasional small sacrifices as well.

The subordinate's calling is not free of all perils either, and we must warn him again, even at the risk of becoming tedious and appearing to preach: *To fully reap the benefits of his station, the subordinate must genuinely and irrevocably be committed to it.* Even a faint and occasional desire to desert subordinate ranks provides a powerful lever for the Superiors to blackmail and to exploit him, and to deprive him of the privileges his position entitles him to. Misdirected and foolish ambition

---

* And let us not assume for a moment that executives are perhaps not men of principle, for many of them are just that, and some will on principle make a deal even on the proposition that two and two equal four.

to mutate into a Superior is a subordinate's Achilles' heel, and steadfast devotion to his subordinate's badge in his armor.

The foregoing description of some of the basic characteristics of subordinate jobs begs the question—If these jobs are so first-rate, and with pluses so heavily outweighing minuses, why is there no cutthroat competition for them, and why is there instead a wild and near-universal scramble for a spot up the executive ladder? The answer, deceptively simple but true is: Common sense is uncommon, vanity is rampant, two birds in the bush are more in demand than one in the hand, and the idolaters of the tinsel of executive success crowd out the enlightened celebrants of the solid worth of subordinate life.

# 2

# Selecting the right subordinate position

> O, let us love our occupations,
> Bless the squire and his relations,
> Live upon our daily rations,
> And always know our proper stations.
> Dickens: *The Chimes*

Jobs, as all elements and some wives, make good servants and bad masters. But here ends similarity with the elements. We do not choose the weather, and there is really not much we can do about it (except maybe move someplace else where the humidity is not so high). At the same time, if we really must get married or take a job, a good initial choice will make a lot of difference. And now that we have neatly disposed of the subjects of weather and matrimony, we can confine our attention in the remainder of this chapter to the selection of subordinate jobs alone.

## EXPERTISE, NOT ABILITY

Some subordinate jobs are better than others in that they make it easier to secure and maintain independence. Consequently, they also provide better leverage in the application of the Radović Rule. It is important, however, to know that, *whatever occupation the subordinate chooses, it is not ability he should demonstrate, but expertise.* (*Expertise* is the real or alleged capacity to do something, presumably acquired through extensive study and practice. *Ability* is the same capacity, usually assumed, and presumably acquired with little or no learning or experience.) Ability makes one promotion-prone, and is therefore treacherous, while expertise is a very stabilizing influence that helps anchor a man to the job he happens to be in.* Direct advertising of one's expertise is one of the recommended methods of building a professional reputation. A subordinate can, to take a specific example, openly and often boast of his great specialized expertise in designing tool crib factory layouts. One acquaintance of this writer, employed in a large metalworking plant, did, and he not only derived much pleasure out of this

---

* The reader may wonder, quite naturally, how difficult it is, and how long does it really take, to become an expert. Let this be the least of his worries: Instant expertise can be acquired effortlessly by anyone through the simple device of smothering the obvious in the irrelevant and the obscure, preferably to the accompaniment of solemn motions and oracular incantations.

but he also, virtually on the basis of verbal claims alone, built an enviable professional reputation that no one ever tried to question, and assured himself of a good job as a tool crib layouts expert for as long as he wanted it. False modesty has no place in the application of the Radović Rule.

*Expertise is best established in some esoteric or narrowly specialized technical field* such as the development of numbering systems for spare parts, the composition of account numbers, registry, archives and library codification work, updating of equipment maintenance manuals, laboratory quality-testing in a single-product large chemical plant, etc. These fields are gingerly approached by Superiors and subordinates alike. A normal executive will not only delegate but gladly altogether relinquish his authority to a numbering systems expert if only to keep the subject matter of the expert's specialty at arm's length. And the prospect of being compelled to fill a vacancy of the kind just described can induce a state of deep depression in many an ill-informed subordinate. Jobs with these and like descriptions are bastions of autonomy for the incumbent.

## THE SUPERIORITY OF UNPOPULAR JOBS

*The less inviting or more repugnant a job appears to be to the uninitiated, the more irreplaceable the subordinate doing it will be considered, and the more independence and job satisfaction he can win for himself.* In a job that is nobody's cup of tea, the incumbent has an unusual opportunity for making it what he really wants

it to be, with a virtual guarantee of immunity from outside interference, and with adequate breaks for various
extracurricular activities which are a legitimate part of
the "job-enrichment" concept (e.g., keeping tab on the
racetrack to add variety to the job content, or dabbling
in real estate to compensate for chronic inequities in
subordinate salary scales). To these activities the subordinate has an inalienable, if sometimes still disputed
right, and he should exercise his right freely and regularly
for, as the Turkish proverb says, "Baklava is not for the
man who likes it, but for the one who is accustomed to
it." Outmoded and reactionary personnel management
concepts notwithstanding, a healthy part of the workday
devoted to hobbies greatly contributes to high employee
morale. And a satisfied work force, as everybody knows,
being the foundation on which a successful organization
stands, the subordinate who by any means available to
him seeks fulfillment at work can rejoice in the knowledge that he is at the same time also helping his employer.

The leverage of a judiciously selected job and the
validity of the Radović Rule are well demonstrated in the
application of the "I am quitting" threat gambit, so dear
to our hearts, and so often resorted to without proper
credentials. A well-placed subordinate can use it with impunity, to finagle some advantage for himself and even,
occasionally, to indulge in a pique. *Any executive hates
to lose an expert who is most difficult to replace and who,
in addition, represents no threat to him.* He may think the
threat is a bluff, but he seldom will dare call it. One
should also add that, for the threat to be effective, indispensability need not be proved, but only implied. The
proper subordinate job, by virtue of the job title alone,

*Any executive hates to lose an expert who is most difficult to replace and who, in addition, represents no threat to him.*

assures this. In contrast, the Superior must daily give
proof or semblance of performance, and endlessly exert
himself just to show that he need not be fired and replaced. (The subordinate "I am quitting" stratagem, by
the way, may look to the casual observer like blackmail—
which, on reflection, it really often is. But, surely, a
resolute subordinate who can keep a steady eye on a
worthy goal beyond the dust cloud of daily trivia will
not be sidetracked and prevented from reaching his intended destination by a silly notion of fair play and by
piddling middle-class moral scruples. And, besides, it is
for the subordinate to go ahead and do what is right for
the subordinate cause, and not to ponder at length the
justification for human actions, because, as a philosopher
wisely reminds us, "man is born to live life, not to understand it.")

## ENOUGH GOOD JOBS TO GO AROUND?

We now have some idea of the kind of job the subordinate should be looking for, but the problem of finding
such jobs still remains. Are there enough of them to
satisfy any demand? On this score we can confidently put
the reader's worries to rest. Such categories of work
abound, as even a superficial survey will disclose. *With
technology on the march,* and its administration more
than keeping step, *there is no danger of the bountiful
supply of seemingly repulsive jobs drying out in the fore-
seeable future.* (Remember the computer, heralded as
the bane of drudgery and the greatest laborsaving device
of all time, which ended up creating many more unpopular jobs than it ever eliminated?) A subordinate with

only modest powers of observation should have no trouble in finding for himself a highly rewarding occupation. The fact that there is neither demand nor competition for such work only shows how little common sense people have, or how uninformed they are.

Good subordinate jobs are never really in short supply, but the pickings are even better than usual when the organization expands, which is a straightforward case that needs no explaining, or when a new reform-minded top-level executive billed as "dynamic," "positive" and "innovating" takes the organization or part of it over. His performance is often an interesting if predictable one: The poor man feels the pressure to live up to his reputation and, noisily flapping his wings like a fattened gander, he tries to take off and show the world how he soars (only to land with a dull thud on his behind three feet farther down the runway). In his infinite widsom, usually born of a swollen head, he fires and hires, switches underlings around, and generally mucks things up, ending with the same old something, freshly stirred. Although he is as effective as the fly in La Fontaine's fable that thought that its buzzing was what moved the horses and the cart, he does often create vacancies in executive ranks which are then partially filled by subordinate turncoats, thus occasionally making available choice assignments in the subordinate bracket.

## A CASE IN POINT

The criteria described in this chapter for selecting subordinate jobs, which boil down to a recommendation to look for seemingly uninviting jobs and acquire an

expertise (real or presumed) in them, may appear unusual and novel. They have, nevertheless, been valid for
at least as long as history goes back in time. There is no
better proof of this than the saga of ancient Babylon's
sanitation workers: By far the best and most renowned
in Mesopotamia (and at a time when sanitation was not
taken for granted as it is today), they contributed in no
small measure to the comparative attractions of daily life
of their sophisticated city. But while keeping Babylon
clean, salubrious, and with nothing to offend the refined
nostrils of its urbane citizens, they also fed the envy of
Babylon's neighbors, Assyrians in particular, whose capital, Nineveh, had no sanitation to speak of. A fetid stench
hung without reprieve over Nineveh, and literally drove
Assyrian kings and their armies out of city walls, with
nothing much to do but engage in military conquest.

Unable to contain their long-simmering envy any
more, the Assyrians, in 689 B.C., unleashed a savage attack
on Babylon, sacked the city, and put its population to the
sword. But Babylon's sanitation men were all spared, on
strict orders from Sennacherib, the Assyrian king. He
offered them better pay, subsidized housing and, among
other fringe benefits, separate and guaranteed seating in
temples and at games, if only they would come and work
in Nineveh. This, of course, was an offer they could not
refuse, and so to Nineveh they went and arrived there
amid great popular rejoicing. Nor did they disappoint
their newly adopted city, for in a very short time they
cleaned it up thoroughly and made of it a place fit to
breathe in. And now the king and his army found life in
Nineveh so much to their liking that they rarely, if ever,
ventured out of it. With Assyrians comfortably ensconced

in their capital, the fear in the hearts of their vassals and enemies gave way to security; security gave way to confidence, confidence to courage, and courage to brazenness, and soon the Assyrians found themselves with a full-scale rebellion on their hands. In 612 B.C., an allied force of Medes and Babylonians (who by now had somewhat recovered politically and militarily, but not sanitation-wise) laid seige to Nineveh, stormed it and slaughtered its citizens or sold them into slavery. But no one laid a finger on our sanitation workers. Both Medes and Babylonians bid for their services, offering them terms even better than those Assyrians had given them. The Medes outbid the Babylonians, and Nineveh's sanitation workers went to their capital, Ecbatana. And there, when in 539 B.C. Ecbatana fell to Cyrus, the Persian king, their story repeated itself again.

The story just told took place more than twenty-five centuries ago, but the situation hasn't changed much since: Sanitation work is still not popular, but the sanitation workers' welfare is still given due consideration, and their demands carry as much weight as ever (and anybody who has lived through a sanitation strike will readily agree with that). The Radović Rule is as valid now as it was then.

# 3

# The use of rules
# and regulatoins

Any fool can make a rule
And every fool will mind it.
Thoreau: *Journal*

Once the subordinate has selected the proper job, he should learn how to use the many weapons inherent in his position. One of the most effective of these weapons at his disposal is the use of rules and regulations, the study of which should be a priority item on his agenda.

No one questions the wisdom of a rule or regulation that has long been in existence. With time, a rule or regulation dissociates itself from the fallibility of its human creator and mysteriously becomes endowed with a dogmalike authority of its own, whether it makes sense or not. In fact, the less sense it makes, the less likely it is to be questioned. Traces of logic in a rule or regulation are telltale signs of its human origin, and thus only tend to undermine its authority and credibility.

But, then, it is not the function of rules and regulations to make sense or, as so-called management experts would have us believe, to make it possible for an organization to perform some alleged service for society at large. The only genuine reason for establishing rules and regulations in an organization is to provide a stable system of interpersonal relationships in which life is predictable and simple, and where there are no dilemmas and dangers as long as the rules and regulations are observed.

Every bureaucracy has, collectively, a vested interest in such havens of security and stability, and any violator caught breaking rules and regulations and disturbing the peace and order of organizational life is prosecuted with all the zeal and fury with which the Inquisition pursued a heretic. No Superior is unaware of this, and his respect for rules and regulations is deep and genuine, and often bordering on awe and worship. The case is known, for instance, of a high Ministry of Finance official, of a government we shall leave unnamed, who would not accept bribes until he assured himself that regulations allowed remuneration for services rendered, from sources other than his employer, of up to 30 percent of his annual Civil Service pay. And then he scrupulously made sure never to go over the 30 percent limit.

The only executive who will break rules and regulations irresponsibly and set precedents is the "raider" type of executive, who typically has not come through the ranks, and who knows of his authority but not of his duties to the organization. He is, fortunately, a comparatively rare and short-lived phenomenon, and the only antidote needed for this irritant is a little patience and Christian forbearance, to give him time and rope enough to hang himself (which he efficiently and invariably does, even without anybody's help). The typical Superior, however, obeys the rules, and plays it safe, like the husband who follows the time-tested advice of the Arab proverb which says "Beat your wife every morning: If you don't know why, she does." But *while the executive seeks the protection of rules and regulations he at the same time, by obeying them, surrenders much of his freedom of action and no subordinate who is aware of this should have trouble running circles around a Superior witlessly hobbled of his own will.* A case history, briefly told, will illustrate what we have in mind:

In the Incoming Mail Unit of a large East Coast utility, the Unit's new supervisor, a certain Mr. Turnipp, was loathed by the mail clerks, and for good reason: He was a fanatic for following proper procedure, a stickler for detail, and he liked nothing better than to look over his subordinates' shoulders and breathe down their necks. For this he had plenty of time as there was nothing else for him to do, except personally to examine, according to the established rule, mail marked "confidential," and decide on its disposition. This he did willingly and without fail because it made him feel important, but there just wasn't enough of this mail to keep him long out of his subordinates' hair. That is, there wasn't enough of it until the day the mail clerks got their heads together and

bought themselves a dozen or so "confidential" stamps
(all of a different type, so as not to arouse suspicion),
and, when Turnipp was not around, started gradually
marking more and more pieces of correspondence with
their newly acquired tools. Within a few months Turnipp,
sitting at his desk behind a large pile of "confidential"
mail that never seemed to get any smaller, had hardly
enough time to go to the men's room and barely took
notice of his staff. He was cursing under his breath and
often wondering aloud why on earth should some pieces of
mail ever have been marked "confidential." But he went
on with his toil, for rules are rules and must be obeyed,
and he did all of it by himself because he certainly was
not about to share his special "privileged" responsibilities
with any of his staff. And so, while the boss was minding
the rules, and doing in the process much of his subordinates' work, the subordinates were taking it easy and
reaping the rewards of a proper use of rules and regulations.

And now, after these general introductory remarks,
we should go back to specifics, to give the reader a few
pointers of practical value. To better achieve this, it might
prove useful to divide our subject matter into some logical
subcategories, as follows:

## WRITTEN RULES AND REGULATIONS

A careful perusal of rules and regulations *in a large
organization* will disclose that *for every conceivable rule
and regulation there is a counterrule and counterregula-
tion,* as if always to provide an escape clause for human

Sitting at his desk behind a large pile of "confidential" mail that never seemed to get any smaller, Turnipp had hardly enough time to go to the men's room.

imperfection and also to reward the diligent student of the science of Management of Superiors. *Almost any decision of a Superior that encroaches on the prerogatives of subordinates can be demonstrated to be in flagrant conflict with some explicit organization rule or regulation.* Without delay, the Superior should be alerted to this, and if he is of genuine executive caliber (and not a rules and regulations expert himself) he can be counted upon to turn around and beat a full retreat.

It would be a grave mistake to underestimate the practical value of the proposition just formulated. This proposition is, in fact, the explanation for the continued existence of much of what the management likes to describe as "feather bedding:" Many a management plan supposedly intended to increase efficiency and cut costs (at the expense of subordinates, of course) has come to nought because it ran afoul of some existing rule or regulation that the rank and file could invoke in defense of their interests, and this is why we have available today such wonderful subordinate jobs as those of firemen on diesel and electric trains, elevator operators in automatic elevators, and, in some places, town criers in this age of TV, radio, and telephone.

But occasionally, even in the largest and oldest organizations, there will be no rule or regulation exactly answering the need of the subordinate. This, however, should not bother him unduly, for as every serious student of the subject well knows, proper interpretation of rules and regulations greatly extends their scope and usefulness. To give an example that easily comes to mind (and that the reader, having probably had personal experience with this sort of thing, will readily recognize), mention

can be made of the flexible interpretation of what con-
stitutes sickness, which assures an employee the full
benefit of his company's sick-leave provisions. Similarly,
an imaginative interpretation of the rules governing the
filing of expense claims assures that sufficient mileage is
gotten out of expense accounts: There is no need for the
subordinate to practice deception (and risk killing the
goose that lays the golden egg), if he knows how to
interpret the truth.

As already explained, the purpose of rules and regulations is to assure stability, which also means to preserve
the status quo. As such, they are particularly suitable for
blocking action, although they occasionally give excellent
results in securing positive action as well. To explain this
in more dynamic terms, the use of rules and regulations in
the application of the Radović Rule is more defensive
than offensive, more in the nature of judo than karate.
The subordinate who, for example, strictly observes the
9–5 office hours, and files his nails in the interval, is less
exposed to executive frame-up than the poor devil who
slaves at his desk but is occasionally late in the morning.
As long as the subordinate's activities can be represented
as sanctioned by rules and regulations he is safe, and is
walking through the treacherous organizational corridors
dressed in impenetrable armor plate.

## UNWRITTEN RULES

The validity of observations made at the beginning
of this chapter is not restricted to written rules and regulations, but applies to unwritten rules and established

practices as well. Not rarely, it is just *because* it is so sacrosanct that an established practice cannot be written up. *If the typical executive has true respect for written rules and regulations, he is often no less than terrified by the unwritten ones.* Can anyone think, for instance, of a Superior with a key to the top management rest room patronizing the rank and file toilet? A thorough knowledge of unwritten practices is an absolute must for a qualified subordinate. It can tell him, to give just one of so many examples, how to bring on, when it suits his purpose, a wholesale top management crisis by simply jamming the lock to one single door.


**PRECEDENTS**

*The executive's fear is also not limited to breaches of existing rules and regulations,* both written and unwritten. *He is equally afraid, if not more, of breaking new ground and establishing a precedent* (and that is why he often likes to run in circles, on a familiar, safe, and well-trodden path). A precedent, while it may not be in conflict with any existing rules and regulations, is also outside their protection, and no executive worth his salt is going to risk his future with a decision he later may be called upon to justify. A subordinate who knows his rules and regulations will very often have no trouble in identifying a harmful decision as a precedent. The offending Superior is then alerted, preferably through a third party, that he is entering dangerous uncharted territory (the key word *precedent* must be pronounced). The decision will be rescinded in no time, and most probably written off as just a misunderstanding. This writer recalls an incident concerning a columnist in a news agency which is a case in point:

The columnist had announced his intention of recommending a raise in pay for one of his research assistants, whose only merit was that he had done his utmost to ingratiate himself with his boss. Hearing of this, the other assistants were understandably furious, but they decided to use their heads rather then give in to their feelings in fighting this sort of blatant favoritism. They made no useless verbal protests and wrote no letters of complaint of dubious value. Instead, they all signed a memorandum to the columnist, lauding his decision to recommend a raise in pay for one of them, and adding that such a pay raise would represent a justified, if belated, recognition of the importance of their responsibilities, and a welcome precedent they fully intended to use in pressing for an upward pay reclassification for all of them. Needless to say, the columnist went back on his word, never made his intended recommendation and was left pondering over some other way of rewarding his by now thoroughly disgruntled favorite.

## A RECOMMENDATION TO THE READER

The preceding text should have left little doubt in the mind of the reader about the great potential of rules and regulations as a tool of Management of Superiors. But whether this potential will be realized will depend entirely on the subordinate's mastery of his own organization's rules and regulations. He should stint no effort in

learning all there is to know about them, for there is no
more rewarding field of study, quite apart from the intrinsic interest of their subject matter. And lest there be
some misunderstanding, we hasten to add that the subordinate should study rules and regulations not better
to obey them, but better to compel the Superior to toe
the organizational line when this is beneficial to the subordinate cause. He himself should use his learning to
sidestep the line whenever needed, and thus make out of
executive hegemony, only more subtly, thoroughly and
efficiently, what the Italians made out of Mussolini's dic-
tatorship—"a tyranny tempered by the complete disregard
of all laws."

   To conclude, we can well nigh guarantee to the subordinate who does his homework well, and is ready to
apply his knowledge, that he will always find corporate
rules and regulations to be one of his most effective instruments of redress in *the Organization*—which, *left to
itself, without corrective measures, will typically lavish
its favors and attention on Superiors and subordinates in
roughly the same proportion the average housewife
divides hers between her fingernails and her toenails.*

**4**

# The company one keeps

Good company and good discourse are the very sinews of
virtue.

Izaak Walton: *The Compleat Angler*

A closetful of Brooks Brothers suits may or may not make
a man, but *one or two known or rumored friends higher
up in the organization always improve the impression an
employee makes.* At the same time, it can be observed
that, like the proverbial lamppost that one man uses for
illumination and another for support, company is also put
to different uses by different people. Some, as the genuine
executive, see in it a tool; others, as the idle rich, only a

toy. For the discerning subordinate, it should be both.
For the subordinate, the pleasures of socializing at work
are legitimate and even recommended, only they should
not be permitted to obscure its functional aspects, as
socializing is also one of the important instruments of the
Radović Rule. He should, in Wall Street parlance, "strad-
dle" his social opportunities and make them work for him
both ways, in the tradition of the girl who shows leg and
bosom to the legal limit but reacts with blushing chaste-
ness or haughty dignity to ogling and wolf whistles.

## WHO THE SUBORDINATE KNOWS
## DOES MATTER TO HIS SUPERIOR

A Superior has usually no interest whatever in the
the connections of his subordinates, no matter how color-
ful they may be, as long as they are outside his orbit of
career interests. Within this orbit, however, his sensitivity
to such connections is most acute (even though he may
not be an Esalen alumnus). *The Superior will take note
in no time of a subordinate's friendliness with any VIPs,*
say, members of the Promotion Committee, his own Superior, or any other highly placed potential benefactor
(or malefactor). His keen mind will immediately recognize, often through a remarkable stretch of imagination,
the bearing such relationship may have on the furthering
of his career.

A friendly greeting from a VIP, not to speak of a
hearty handshake or a slap on the back bestowed by a top
executive on the subordinate and witnessed by the Superior, will definitely set the subordinate in a class by

*A friendly handshake from a VIP, bestowed on the subordi-nate and witnessed by the Superior, will set the subordinate in a class by himself.*

himself where he can do no wrong in the eyes of his supervisor: A man so anointed by top management must have some very special qualities, however well hidden they may be.

*The subordinate whose social worth has been recognized by his Superior will receive very special consideration.* He will not only be treated with undue courtesy and friendliness, but will soon be taken into the confidence of his Superior, who knows the value of cultivating sources of information that supposedly filters up to the top.

The subordinate should, therefore, carefully tend to the human values of his working environment: His Superior's career may depend on it (or at least the Superior seems to think so). The realization that, if one looks at things this way, it is really not his own but his Superior's interests that are at stake will give the subordinate a psychological advantage in enhancing his public relations. He will acquire a certain air of detachment that will not be lost on VIPs. It will soon become evident to them that here is a man of integrity and independence of mind who wants only to enjoy the company of his fellow men, and has no intention of exploiting them for his own promotion. This certainly will be rewarded by more noticeable and useful greetings, more hearty handshakes, and even more frequent friendly slaps on the back.


## NAME-DROPPING

*The usefulness of simple name-dropping as a tool of Management of Superiors,* it must be said, *is greatly overrated.* It is true that the Superior will usually be inclined to play it safe and give the subordinate the benefit of the doubt even for inept and gauche name-dropping. But it is even more true that the sound of a name dropped can never match for effect the visual impact of a full-fledged VIP abrazo or the credentials of an office rumor reported by a third, disinterested party.

*If name-dropping must be engaged in,* either because of a dearth of other means, or because of sheer compulsion, it is well to remember that *its effectiveness will be considerably enhanced if the Superior learns of the subordinate's impressive social contacts through somebody else rather than from the subordinate himself.* Truth is not self-evident, it is established by witnesses.

## THERE IS ALWAYS A WAY

A subordinate may not know anybody in high places and may not be adept at name-dropping, but this should not discourage him if he is aware, intuitively or otherwise, of the practical implications of the Radović Rule. Witness the case of Henry Spaniel, an accounting clerk for a large life insurance company, who early in his career could not list a name of a VIP even among his nodding acquaintances. To make up for this deficiency, Henry Spaniel conceived a simpleminded, yet quite effective little scheme. Regularly, twice a year, he would rent a chauffered black Cadillac (for half an hour at a time) to pick him up at the company's front door at office closing time. In the car would be waiting a pal of his with a conspicuous and imposing physique of 290 pounds, attired in his Sunday suit, and with wraparound sunglasses and a lit cigar. The mysterious tycoon in his Cadillac, naturally, generated much curiosity, but Henry wasn't talking. To only two carefully selected articulate friends in the office he confided, after exacting from them an oath of secrecy, that the man was a very important stockholder and a Director of many corporations who needed grass-roots information on the company's management. These days, Henry Spaniel can often be seen gracefully accepting a ride offered by a VIP in his company's own chauffered black Cadillac. He also needs no dummy high-level contacts any more, for he now has real ones.

# 5

# Keeping the Superior insecure and off-balance

Neurosis seems to be a human privilege.
Sigmund Freud: *Moses and Monotheism*

Fear, clinically also known as insecurity, has been with man since time immemorial, and is likely to stay with him till doomsday. This being the case, we might as well resign ourselves to this affliction, and make the most of it. The psychoanalysts, judging by their fees, already have.*

---

* And the psychoanalytic practice today would have been even more prosperous than it already is except for the healthy belief and spreading realization among the educated young that whenever something goes wrong it is never they who are to blame, but always someone else: With more and more of the people being right all the time, and knowing it, the psychoanalyst's couch may soon become a thing of the past.

While there is no need, for the purposes of the analysis in this chapter, to delve into any general aspects of psychology and psychopathology, the specialized subject of executive neuroses is of particular concern to this book: *Executive neuroses are not of medical interest only, but have considerable management significance as well* and, for the asking, the subordinate can share in the bonanza they are capable of yielding. However, to better understand how, we should start from the beginning.

By the very nature of his position and of his ambitions the Superior is insecure. Around the clock, and all at the same time, he longs to move ahead, fears attacks from the rear and is on the alert for hostile, outflanking maneuvers. The executive who under these circumstances can keep his peace of mind has rare qualities indeed or, more likely, has little sense. Normally, he has no equanimity whatsoever, and his career hopes and fears make him respond readily to well-designed subordinate pressures, not to say manipulation. True, he usually develops all kinds of defense mechanisms, some obvious, some in disguise, but none without a chink.*

*The condition of insecurity in the Superior is the very cornerstone of Management-of-Superiors strategy, and no effort should be spared to bring it about and to maintain it, but at a correct level.* For this the subordinate must develop a fine sense of balance and timing. He must not make the Superior insecure to the extent of

---

* For example, the Socratic method of problem-solving, typical of many a bureaucrat, of confronting every issue with an unending stream of irrelevant questions for fear that if he stops he might have to do something with the answers. The proper countermethod is not to rebel under questioning, but to obligingly swamp him with a deluge of even more irrelevant answers.

getting him, so to say, over the brink and into irrational behavior, and yet he must not lull him into a feeling of security that will lead to cocky self-confidence and negative patterns of behavior. Only if a correct level of insecurity is maintained in the Superior can he be counted upon to respond with highly predictable, quasi-Pavlovian reflexes to a subordinate applying the stimuli of the Radović Rule.

In simple terms, this means that the overconfident Superior must have his confidence shaken, while the overly diffident one must on the contrary have his boosted. Ideally, if the analogy may be permitted, in the curious Superior-subordinate relationship that can be described but not always explained, the Superior should ever be made to feel like that Roman poet of old who wrote to his wife "I can live neither with you nor without you." In this state of mind, which is a delicate mixture of faint hope, resignation and exasperation (and which is, chances are, not unknown to the married male reader), the Superior is, as our Rule has already implied, the perfect medium for the subordinate to work with. We shall now see how this state of mind can be elicited, whether the subordinate has to contend with an overconfident Superior, or with an overly discouraged one.


## THE OVERCONFIDENT EXECUTIVE

When overconfident, the Superior, as any normal human being, will tend to become obnoxious, will monopolize conversation, use subordinates as captive audience and the like. He even may begin to indulge in the nar-

cissistic exercise of power over his subordinates for its
own sake. Still worse, he will try to size up his subordinate, to reduce him to a known quantity so he can use
him more readily in his own equation for success. Or, to
put it more simply, the oversecure Superior will inevitably
begin to plot his next move up the executive ladder and,
inevitably again, will find a place for the subordinate in
these plans. Now, this absolutely must not be allowed to
take place, as it is the exact opposite of that which the
application of the Radović Rule is supposed to achieve.
*The overconfident Superior must be kept psychologically
off terra firma and on slippery ground, where he can be
tripped as needed.*

There are numerous ways and opportunities for trimming down excesses of executive security and self-
reliance, and the subordinate of only average resourceful-
ness will have no difficulty in identifying or devising
them, and making sure that his Superior will always approach him with at least a touch of proper and useful
nervousness (like the man looking down the barrel of a
supposedly empty gun: probably safe, but uncomfort-
able), if not downright apprehension. For illustration,
we shall now give several examples of such corrective
action, applied to some typical executive specimens
guilty, among other things, of over-confidence.

Many an executive routinely and confidently pretends, for the benefit of his own Superiors, to know all
the details and intricacies of the work done by his subordinates (and better than the subordinates themselves)
and, sometimes, even to have done it himself. He also
seldom heeds the advice given by Lord Keynes that "it
is better to keep one's mouth shut and seem ignorant,

*There are numerous ways and opportunities for trimming down excesses of executive security and self-reliance.*

than to open it and remove all doubt." In order to demonstrate his sure grasp and mastery of his job and convey this illusion to his peers and higher-ups he will, however, usually have enough sense to pump his subordinates for information before an executives' meeting, and ask them for briefing notes and summary reports. Without these briefings and notes the sum total of his knowledge on matters to be discussed often equals zero, and in this inherent dependence of the Superior on the subordinate for fake expertise lies a golden opportunity for the subordinate to deflate a puffed-up Superior and make him much more receptive to the dominant management role of the subordinate.

This is a situation the subordinate should capitalize on, as the Assistant to the Controller in a Minneapolis-St. Paul furniture company did: The Controller of the company, to listen to the man himself talking with self-assured bluff, was a great financial expert and a wizard at figures, but when it came to actual work, it was his Assistant who really did it all. Moreover, four times a year, every year, the hapless young man had to coach the Controller for two or three full days on end, just to enable him to make a simple presentation of the Balance Sheet and the Income Statement at the quarterly meeting of the Board of Directors. For his toil, the Assistant never got any raise, recognition or thanks from his boss, but knowing no better and being meek by nature, he never made much fuss about being so badly used. Then, one early spring, just a few days before the quarterly meeting of the Board of Directors, the Assistant had a painful attack of kidney stones and, on strict doctor's orders, had to absent himself from work for an entire week. The

Controller, having no choice, tried to prepare the financial statements by himself, made a mess of it, botched miserably the presentation to the Board by knowing too little and talking too much, and missed being fired by the skin of his teeth. On his return to the office the Assistant found his boss a changed man: considerate, humble, almost diffident, concerned about his Assistant's well-being, and willing to consider a raise in pay. The Assistant quickly pieced the new picture together, saw the light, and then made sure the change was permanent by regularly mentioning recurring kidney-stone troubles at about the times the Board of Directors was due to meet.

Everybody knows the executive whose specialty soapbox is loyalty to organization, perched on top of which he loudly, confidently and regularly exhorts and bullies his subordinates to greater efforts and dedication to work.* This executive must be given the opportunity to practice what he preaches, and to provide a shining example for those he leads. The recommended *modus operandi* is the one that was chosen for the Chief Engineer of a large construction company by his smart subordinates: They volunteered his name as chairman of the company's annual blood-donor campaign knowing well that the man fainted at the sight of blood, but remembering that he also once said that "civic-mindedness is expected of every man on the payroll of this Company." They delayed passing on to him "rush" matters till 5 P.M., or accumulated them for late Friday afternoon, mindful of the fact that he often used to remind them that "overtime is a right of the Com-

---

* He is, incidentally, usually easy to recognize by his executive "Uphill on the Bicycle" stance: treading hard on his subordinates while bowing low to his Superiors.

pany to ask, and a duty of the employee to perform."
They planned for emergencies to occur during his vacations but made sure to know where he could be reached
and called back to the office, because he was fond of re-
peating that "vacations must not and will not interfere
with the work in this Organization." And they did other
things like that to him. This treatment had a strange
cooling effect on the Chief Engineer. He soon began to
feel the chill of insecurity even when fully wrapped in
the company flag, and it was not long before he gave up
importuning his subordinates with unreasonable demands
and highfalutin talk.

Another overconfident character is the "Charging
Bull" type of Superior, the clatter of whose hooves con-
tinuously disturbs the quiet of working hours. He is best
taken care of with the *muleta* ploy, by draping over in
red the entrance to the lion's den. An interesting example of this ploy in action is the little-remembered
"Pasta and Fagioli Affair" in sixteenth-century Florence:

The late 1530s were years of dark intrigue, plots and
murders at the court of the Medicis in Florence, where
everybody distrusted and feared everybody else. Cosimo
I de Medici (later known as Cosimo the Great) was still
a young man, barely past twenty, and to ease the strains
of his office he often went hunting in the Tuscan country-
side, a falcon perched on his left fist. With him usually
went a large retinue, consisting of young noblemen (executives of that time), ladies of the court, guards and
servants, and the dwarf, Panino, the court jester (an
indispensable subordinate post at any self-respecting
feudal court). The noblemen were a motley crew of dis-
solute, overbearing and truculent rowdies, and one of the

worst among them was a certain Pietro de Fagioli, a cocksure hothead and a callous kiss-and-tell gallant, bent more on the telling than on the kissing. Another among these sidekicks of Cosimo was one Giorgio della Pasta, and between him and de Fagioli there was not much love wasted, on account of some earlier quarrel over money. Panino felt a deep hared for de Fagioli, not only because he was often the butt of de Fagioli's crude practical jokes, but even more because de Fagioli, just to win a bet, had seduced and then made fun in public of a trusting young maid in the Medici household, one of the few people that was ever kind to poor Panino.

Panino swore that he would avenge her, and as things turned out, he didn't have to wait long for it: During one of the hunting outings, after a strenuous morning in the saddle, Cosimo's hunting party stopped at one of his country estates. Following a copious meal, the company broke up and dispersed to the various rooms of the big country house. Some went to take a nap, others to dally, and others again to swap tall stories. De Fagioli was among the last, bragging as usual about his latest romantic conquest. A lady of the court, he swore, was madly in love with him, had eyes only for him and would yield to him whenever he felt he wanted her.

"Then," Panino, who was also present, whispered in his ear, "why is she holed up with Giorgio della Pasta in the room at the end of the corridor?" Having said this, Panino ducked under the table (as a bearer of bad news is usually well advised to do), and de Fagioli, stung to the quick and livid with rage, jumped to his feet and, dagger in hand, ran out of the room and up the corridor to do della Pasta in. But there was a guard standing in front of the door, and he did his noisy very best to prevent de Fagioli from breaking in. Cosimo, for it was he who was in the room taking an afternoon siesta, woke up, and convinced that this was an attempt on his life, didn't bother to dress and investigate (being an essentially practical man), but jumped out of the window and, stark naked, took off for the nearest bushes. But he was soon flushed out of there by a pack of dogs belonging to some boys from the nearby village who were gathering berries and mushrooms in the woods. To escape from this new peril, Cosimo the Great shinnied up a tree, and that is where his men found him that evening, shivering from the cold, with a badly mortified pride, and in a murderous mood. In the meantime, they also had overpowered de Fagioli, and held him in custody for Cosimo to decide his fate. The evidence against de Fagioli was overwhelming. He had gravely wounded the soldier guarding Cosimo's door, had broken into Cosimo's room, and was found there, bloodied dagger in hand. Cosimo, in no frame of mind to listen to de Fagioli's explanations and protestations of innocence, had him garrotted, Spanish fashion, on the spot, just as Panino had expected he would.

Hopefully, the subordinate these days need not use such drastic measures as Panino's, but the effectiveness of the *muleta* ploy in eliminating or undercutting an executive bully is as great today as it was in the past.

Occasionally, a cocky Superior will also be preoccupied with the idea of being known as a nice guy. He either believes popularity is the key to success, or has a congenital need to be liked by others, or both. Naturally, he always needs a scapegoat, a fall guy, or a hatchet man, to take the blame or do the dirty work for him. A deputy or an executive assistant is a natural for this job, but they also are executives of sorts and no concern of ours. However, going down the formal executive chain of command, we reach the rather obnoxious junior executive obsessed with thoughts of great popularity, who has no deputy or assistant, and no one other than a genuine subordinate to turn to and ask to hold the lightning rod for him. This, of course, is our business (and his tough luck), and the solution we usually recommend is for the subordinate to oblige, take the lightning rod manly in both hands and then ground it to the seat of the Superior's pants. This tends to shake the latter up somewhat:

In the data-processing unit of a Detroit area medium-size metal-fabricating plant that specialized in automobile parts, there was an Assistant to the Chief of the unit with marked executive ambitions, an agressive, self-assured young man eager to impress his Superiors and move ahead in the organization, but at the same time careful not to run afoul of the Unions and encounter resistance to his climb from that quarter. He doggedly cultivated both sides of the street but, being too obvious in his attempts to win all-around approval, without much apparent success. Nevertheless, as he could not think of anything better, he persisted in doing things his same old way.

At one point he got the notion that the output of the keypunch subunit was too low, and could be easily raised if keypunch operators would spend less time in the ladies' room gossiping and powdering their noses. But he had no proof that this was so, and he was not about to risk the ire of the operators by conducting a time study on the subject. So he started looking for somebody else to get him the needed information, preferably without the girls being aware of it. He slyly befriended a clerical trainee whose desk was situated not far from the ladies' room, and after lavishing special attention on him for a week or so, took the lad into his confidence and asked him to time and take notes on the ladies' room's in-and-out traffic. The trainee readily agreed, but proved himself to be genuine subordinate material, with an innate feel for the Radović Rule: When, at the end of the day, the Assistant to the Chief came around to his desk and in a low, conspiratorial voice asked him whether he had the information requested, the trainee brightly piped up, "Sure, I timed them, and I made them all sign in and out, and when they protested I told them it was your orders, and to go complain to the union business agent if they wanted."

We hear that the Assistant to the Chief of the data-processing unit keeps very much to himself these days, and has given up trying to enlist the help of the rank and file in hatching his bright ideas.

## THE OVERLY INSECURE EXECUTIVE

When a Superior's voice turns chronically high-pitched or shrill, when he develops a facial tick, when he becomes habitually truculent, or easily breaks down and weeps, it is an indication that he has become too insecure. *In an overly insecure condition, the Superior is unpredictable and therefore difficult to control, and a degree of self-confidence must be quickly restored to him.* This can easily be achieved by softly encouraging him to talk and solicitously listening to him, by preparing for his signature letters on strictly noncontroversial matters, or by asking for his advice on problems which have an obvious and easy solution. *The cure, of course, must not be carried too far,* and the carrot must be withdrawn before the patient becomes obstreperous.

If the Superior happens to be a spelling expert,* the remedy for the morale crisis is obvious and simple: A few spelling errors are put on purpose in whatever is given to him for signature, and a few extra commas are thrown in for good measure. He immediately notices this, and pounces on the opportunity to make an important management contribution. As he tears through the text stalking spelling errors and expunging surplus commas, his flagging spirit is visibly buoyed and he discovers afresh some purpose in life. The number of errors and extra commas left in the text must be carefully measured, however, not to induce executive overconfidence.

---

* A very common species. Often the product of unfulfilled childhood spelling-bee ambitions. Distinguishing characteristics: good grounding in spelling; claiming expertise in grammar and syntax; strong aspirations to literary style. Has a mind keen as a razor blade, with horizon of matching breadth. A born proofreader.

**6**

# Tensions, frictions and suspicions among Superiors

If few can stand a long war without deterioration of soul, none can stand a long peace.

Oswald Spengler: *The Hour of Decision*

To trust others is to be regularly deceived; not to trust them, to be only occasionally outmaneuvered. On the whole, although this is not much of a choice, most people would rather risk the latter than the former, and the Superior is no exception to this rule.

The Superior does not customarily trust his subordinates, but it is his fellow executives whom he really distrusts. There are few dastardly actions or intentions he will consider beyond them or beneath them, maybe not entirely without reason. A normal executive shows a strong predisposition to a persecution complex and, as often as not, it is already in full blossom. *This executive persecution complex, when correctly oriented, is a very healthy phenomenon from the subordinate point of view, and deserves attentive and continuous cultivation.*

## GUIDING THE SUPERIOR'S
## ATTENTION AND ENERGIES

The disposition and preoccupations of the Superior being what they are, *the least the subordinate can do is to give the Superior friendly assistance in detecting a few more snares, plots, intrigues and conspiracies his fellow executives have in store for him.* The perils uncovered need not be imminent, probable or even possible. What they lack in plausibility they will more than make up in credibility. It is also useful to suggest a few ways of countering the supposed maneuveurs of other Superiors. A good piece of advice, for instance, is that attack is the best defense. If heeded, it assures that the executives' energies are channeled in the right direction (away from the subordinate) and usefully spent, and it provides for a good sideshow as well.

The following case history is only one example of how to fully and usefully absorb the attention of executives with one another: Harry Pelican, a quality control inspector in a large Massachusets compo-type (sole cemented to the upper) shoe factory, was thoroughly and understandably fed up with his supervisor, Mr. Hornbill,

*The least the subordinate can do is to give the Superior friendly assistance in detecting a few more snares, plots, intrigues, and conspiracies his fellow executives have in store for him.*

the head of the Brown Men's Shoes Department, who used to spend most of his waking hours closely checking the work of his subordinates. One day, as Mr. Hornbill was playing his regular lunch-hour game of darts with the English-born Mr. Partridge-Grouse, chief of the Black Men's Shoes Department, Harry innocently dropped the rumor that the two of them were the leading candidates to succeed Mr. Livingston "Stork" van Loon, manager of the Men's Shoes Division. The pairing of the two was most felicitous, for they were old friends, and knew enough about each other to last them as ammunition for a lifetime of executive infighting.

In due time, Mr. van Loon was presented with the testimonial silver shoehorn for fifty years of faithful, unselfish and most distinguished service with the company, retired, and replaced (as the President had planned all along) with a highly qualified executive, fresh out of Possum Creek Junior College, who also just happened to be the President's nephew and in need of a job. But Hornbill knew that, except for Partridge-Grouse's scheming and backstabbing (for that, he had no doubts, is certainly what a competitor would do), he would have gotten van Loon's job, and Partridge-Grouse knew the same of Hornbill. As of the writing of this book, the two are still indefatigably pecking at each other and getting more and more even, which leaves Mr. Hornbill precious little time to annoy Harry Pelican. But now we must leave them, idly priming themselves in mutual indignation, and turn our attention to a few other important facets of our subject matter.

## MAINTAINING THE BALANCE
## OF POWER AMONG EXECUTIVES

Continuous intramural battles on the executive front assure a fluid organizational setup, in which the interests of the alert subordinate, prepared to take advantage of career opportunities, are best served. In a stable, and therefore restrictive, power and organization framework, no matter how enlightened the policies it may reflect, the principles of the Radović Rule are more difficult to apply. *But to bring about and preserve this fluid organizational climate favorable to the interests of the subordinate, a balance of power among executives must prevail*, a system of checks and balances must be present. It is in assuring these conditions that genuine statesmanship in a subordinate has the unique opportunity to come to the fore.

While at first it may appear desirable that an amicably disposed management faction or a friendly executive should prevail, the longer-view perspective and past experience warn that no faction or individual, however well-intentioned, should ever be allowed to have complete sway over the lot of others in the organization. Such discretionary power endangers the very foundation on which the strength of the subordinate position is built. In wars of executive hegemony there must be no total and final victory or defeat, lest the integrity of the subordinate cause be jeopardized. When the balance of power in an organization is dangerously tipped to one side, the intelligent subordinate will rise above his personal likes and dislikes and endeavor to restore it, by throwing his support, in his usual discreet and unobtrusive manner ("A

roaring lion catches no game," warns a Uganda saying),
to the losing side.* It will help him, in making the right
decision, always to remind himself that the subordinate
cause, as Palmerston's England, has no eternal friends
and no eternal enemies, but only eternal interests. Or, if
his mind runs more to the down-to-earth, let him just
remember W. C. Fields' pithy dictum "Never give a
sucker an even break."

## BENEFITS TO THE SUBORDINATE

The benefits of keeping the Superior's mind occupied
with executive plotting and maneuvering are many. Most
importantly, *the more the Superior's attention is captured
by the skirmishes and wars of executive life, the more
time the subordinate has to devote to his own professional
and other interests and activities without outside meddling, and to fashion his job to his own specifications.* It
leaves him free and undisturbed to combine the best
features of the corporate system and of entrepreneurship.

## A WORD OF ADVICE

To acquire a taste for participation in executive war-
fare, and *to play the game of goading one executive*

---

* Of course, this is easier said than done. Most of us have strong impulses and biases which affect our behavior, and a man often becomes
objective, equitable and rational only with old age, as in the case of the
old Finnish sailor who once told this writer: "When I was young I was
foolish, and I hated the Russians. Now," he said "now I hate everybody."

*against another for the pleasure of the game itself is potentially dangerous.* It may needlessly expose the unwary subordinate to sudden fire from all sides. Executives are usually at one another's throat without anybody's prodding, and well enough should be left alone. The fire should not be stoked for the idle pleasure of watching the sparks, but only when it is in danger of petering out. The Radović Rule should be used, not abused.

**7**

# On giving credit and showing proper respect

> Do not keep the alabaster boxes of your love and tenderness sealed up until your friends are dead. Fill their lives with sweetness. Speak approving, cheering words while their ears can hear them, and while their hearts can be thrilled and made happier by them.
>
> G. W. Childs: *A Creed*

Man will first speak belittlingly of his fellow men, and will then, just to impress them and gain the sort of recognition he longs for, sit for two months on end perched on top of a pole, or spend his lifetime savings on a hair transplant or a face lift. By thinking that he impresses others, man probably best impresses himself.

## FORMS AND AIMS OF RECOGNITION

*The two basic forms of recognition that the subordinate need know about are the positive, booster-type recognition, and the negative, deflator-type recognition.* The purpose of the first one, better known as praise, is to soften up the Superior in preparation for some demand or jolting surprise the subordinate has in store for him, or to revive him when he is so dispirted that he does not properly respond to the subordinate's proddings. The second one, which also goes under the descriptive names of the "needle" and the "squelch" (and, by the way, is unlikely ever to be recognized as recognition by any Superior), is for bringing high-flying executives down to earth, within the reach of the subordinates applying the Radović Rule and occasionally (but in the name of charity not too often) for the harmless amusement of the latter. It is often best given not straight, but with a thin coating of positive recognition (i.e., praise), which makes it go down easier, and in addition often leaves the Superior confused and even bewildered—a most desirable condition of the executive mind, from the subordinate's point of view. Actual examples of recognition in action as a tool of Management of Superiors will be found a little further in this chapter.

*The subordinate has no need to spend much time devising subtle forms of recognition. The main thing is to give it.* Most executives can be, as the French so descriptively and aptly put it, *assomés à coups d'encensoir*, or roughly translated "beaten senseless with compliments," without ever noticing it. And we all know how difficult to offend some of them are. The more delicate, often time-consuming forms of recognition can be engaged in for the aesthetic pleasure of the subordinate himself, to satisfy his artistic bent, but there is some risk that the effort may be totally lost on the Superior, who much better recognizes the direct, workmanlike approach, being an action-oriented rather than a reflective man. These forms are just one of those things, as the beauty of the *Mikado's* Katisha, that not everyone can see and appreciate.

## COMBINING ETHICS AND PRAGMATISM

*The Superior*, if not always an achiever, is at least a would-be achiever, and in either case *craves positive recognition* more than most people. *To get it, he depends heavily on the subordinate* (it being seldom likely that recognition will come from any other quarter), *and is willing and ready to pay a good price for it.* These being the circumstances, the subordinate must not, like a dope pusher, take unfair advantage of the Superior's addict condition, but neither should he ignore the legitimate opportunities for benefiting himself that the situation affords. He is not bound by the Hippocratic Oath, but there is the subordinate ethic and, in the same way that the oath just mentioned does not rule out profit, *the subordinate ethic does not frown on the subordinate who helps himself by helping his Superior along.* He can be high-minded and practical at the same time, not unlike the girl who stoutly maintained that she was a true romantic (all women do), even allowing that she was quite fond of flowers, and then added emphatically and with feeling, "but I love fresh vegetables."

Secure in the knowledge that "he who giveth, receiveth," and that he is not making a donation but an investment, the subordinate should also not worry about his endeavors being variously described as flattery, adulation, insinuation, ingratiation or by some other such, more colloquial name.* These unfair criticisms are only expressions of envy for work well and successfully done.

The question whether the Superior deserves recognition or not should not trouble the subordinate either because it is irrelevant. It makes no more sense than a doctor asking whether a patient has earned the right to medical attention or not. The only valid question is—does the Superior need recognition treatment? The answer, in ninety-nine cases out of a hundred, is yes, he does. Enough to make it worth the subordinate's time.

## THE CURATIVE PROPERTIES OF RECOGNITION

*The curative properties of recognition, when it is administered to a Superior, cannot be exaggerated.* For instance, an executive, limp with despondence over his past track record and his future prospects, fairly dripping with *Weltschmerz*, and hardly responding to any management stimuli, will make an amazing recovery with an adequate injection of praise. In no time he will be back in proper mental and emotional shape to play the part

---

* "Dogs bark," says a Serbian proverb "and the wind blows the bark away."

assigned to him by the Radović Rule. In the same vein, a boisterous, cocksure Superior subjected to negative recognition will quickly simmer down, ready to take the lead of the subordinate docilely in following a path the latter has charted for him. It is in this application, *as a general conditioning tonic* that makes the Superior more receptive to further specific treatment (e.g., the application of rumors, the insinuation of suspicions and frictions, the selective and timely mention of company rules and regulations, etc.), that *recognition finds its most important use* in the Management of Superiors by subordinates.

*Recognition is a wonderful medicine but, as with any other medication, dosage is of utmost importance.* A completely discouraged Superior is of little use to his subordinate, but one overflowing with self-confidence can be a positive nuisance. In rationing praise, the subordinate must always exercise care and control, and never be carried away by the spectacle of the Superior's appetite: When it comes to compliments, a Superior's intake capacity is like that of a Calcutta bus—there is always room for one more. By the same token, the subordinate must not, by applying his needle, take all the wind out of his Superior's sail and leave him there, inert and good for nothing. Unfortunately, there is no way of prescribing, as one can on a medicine bottle, the exact recognition dose required, and the decision on this must be left to the subordinate's judgment and experience, and to his evaluation of how much recognition his executive patient needs or can take.

## MAXIMIZING RETURNS

Respect being in short supply these days, *positive recognition given before others, and thus subject to the "multiplier effect," is held in particularly high esteem among Superiors.* Negative recognition, of course, does not find the same kind of favor with them, but it is, nevertheless, also subject to the "multiplier effect." The opportunities should not, therefore, be missed to take advantage of occasions to give recognition in public to one's Superior when a strong dose of recognition is needed. For instance, toasting him at the office Christmas party as the one man who finds all the fulfillment he needs in his work, and does not give a hoot about not having made the year's list of promotions; or leading the applause to liven up the Superior's speeches, especially in spots where no one else, somehow, seems to see the reason to join in. The Superior will blush at all this outpouring of recognition, but it may be out of sheer pleasure.

## THE USE OF DISRESPECT

There was a time, not so long ago, when respect for one's Superiors, as respect for one's elders, was the norm, something expected as a matter of course. What people said and showed was necessarily what they felt, the system was not perfect, but somehow it worked.

Today, things are much changed (and apologies to the reader for stating the obvious). In the name of a newly found social concern, love of sincerity and in-

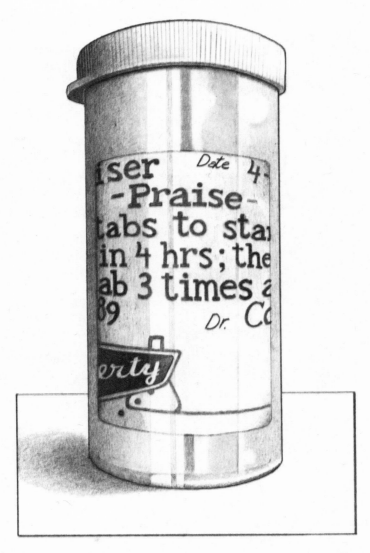

*Recognition is a wonderful medicine but, as with any other medication, dosage is of utmost importance.*

tolerance of hypocrisy, breaches of etiquette and lack of respect for one's seniors have become stock behavior, and the unfriendly, strong-armed, rudely vocal and militant approach to the Management of Superiors is now all too common. On the whole, we do not endorse it. Not that there is anything wrong with verbal abuse and violence in principle, but they just seem always to appear only when imagination fails, or where there was none to begin with. Still, this is no reason enough to reject violence outright in all its forms and ramifications. Violence, or rather the implied threat of it, can occasionally find a useful application.

For instance, take the case of the mousy, timorous executive who has crawled into his position in the wake of a VIP patron, and desperately tries to hold onto it by jumping out of everybody's way, by agreeing with everyone, by asking higher-ups where to scratch when he itches, and by hedging his opinions (if he has any) like a weather forecaster. Often with a face and a personality to guarantee instant oblivion and permanent anonymity, he unobtrusively blends into the background, is sometimes difficult even to detect, and likes it that way. His nerves are usually none too good, and the mere thought of raised voices and confrontations leaves him in cold sweat. On occasion even a toothy smile will scare him away. *A militant posture in the subordinate*, it must be admitted, *is often the most efficient ploy in tending to the shy* (and rather rare) *variety of Superior* just described, because it keeps him effectively in line, and makes him often yield to the subordinate's demands even before they are actually made. It is only an innocent put-on, and it earns good interest without principal.

## RECOGNITION IN ACTION—A FEW EXAMPLES

Recognition finds a very useful application in dealing with the meddling type of Superior who monitors every move of his subordinates and likes to leave his imprimatur on everything, from a request for paper clips to a decision on the location of the office pencil sharpener. The recommended therapy is the following:

Having diagnosed the ability and recognized the achievements of his Superior, the subordinate firmly resolves to get every possible benefit from the Superior's unusual wisdom, knowledge and experience, and to alert others as well to this unique opportunity. He haunts the Superior's office for advice on whether to suppress a comma or not, on whether to write "needs" or "in need of," and follows him on the way to lunch or home to obtain priceless background information on matters of similar importance. He also advertises the Superior and builds him up as the foremost expert on subjects the Superior knows nothing about, and untiringly directs all queries on these subjects to the latter. He nominates the Superior for Treasurer of the Credit Union or for fire-alarm drill captain, and campaigns doggedly for his election. And the like. This sort of recognition invariably brings out in the Superior unsuspected qualities of modesty. He is soon barricaded in his office, and furtively ventures out of it only after making sure his admiring and irrepressible fan is not in sight. He also has lost any visible interest in whatever his subordinate is supposed to do on the job and is only too happy to leave the subordinate alone.

Then, there is the executive the floor of whose office is badly dented from dropping heavy names. Quite often this compulsive activity of his is only a telltale side effect of what is medically known as the "Black-and-Blue Chest Condition," brought on by relentless chest thumping. This affliction is in turn usually accompanied by a severe cranial tension which is the result of an ego much too big for the size of the sufferer's head (and leaving no space in it for any thought and concern for the sub-ordinates' welfare).

The treatment? You have guessed it—laudatory Chinese acupuncture, to bring down the pressure in the head and numb the simian chest-thumping impulses: "Chief, both you and I *know* that you are absolutely brilliant and the pride of our organization, even if we can't quite impress this on anybody else." Or: "I agree a hundred percent with you that our sales performance is rotten, and I have told the General Sales Manager that if he wants to find out what is wrong with his thinking, there is no better man than you to tell him." And so forth. Recognition of the kind just described, administered at frequent intervals, will not fail to let a good deal of gas out of the Superior, to soon put an end to his nonstop paean of self and to make his ear much more receptive to the tunes which the subordinate calls.

The subordinate needn't go out of his way to laud his Superior, because occasions for legitimate praise will present themselves often enough. Even a Superior un-possessed of any admirable qualities must have some redeeming features, or will occasionally do something praiseworthy (at least by accident, if not otherwise). This the subordinate should loudly acknowledge, to generate IOUs for future collection, if not out of goodness of heart.

Sometimes, though, try as one may, pure praise is just not possible. But even then, given the phenomenon that so many people would rather be booed than go unrecognized, mixed recognition (i.e., positive-negative) is much better than nothing at all. "Why, Mr. Primrose," said a pretty secretary to a bald, fat, middle-aged nonentity of a supervisor who, for some time already, had been pursuing her with amorous advances, and had just tried to impress her with his he-man qualities by dressing down an office boy, for no other apparent reason, in front of her, "but for the mane, you are a real lion."

# 8

# Information management
# and the intelligence leaks

The feeble tremble before opinion, the foolish defy it, the
wise judge it, the skillful direct it.

Mme. Roland

*In an organization, wisdom follows the law of gravity: It
always comes from above.* Advice coming from any other
direction, however sensible and to the point, falls at best
on deaf ears.

The above is a basic consideration the subordinate
must keep in mind in approaching data management as
a tool of Management of Superiors. Data management, or
the use of information to achieve results, takes a great

many forms, too many to even mention in one short
chapter, but they all have something in common: The
principle just enunicated in the paragraph above applies
to all of them. Translated into functional terms this means
that *information, to achieve its intended effect, must first
reach a correct destination. If it is also presented in a
suitable shape it will then surely be acted upon.* But, it
would not be fair to ask the reader to accept this principle
just on faith, and some further elaborations on it and
illustrative examples will now be provided.


## AIMING INFORMATION FOR RESULTS

It seldom helps the subordinate to talk reason to his
Superior, especially if there is no profit in it for the
latter.* But reason or not, when the message is from
above, the Superior's receptivity to another man's thinking is greatly improved. If the subordinate has trouble
getting through to his Superior, it is often only because
he has been talking to the wrong man, i.e., the Superior
himself. As any amateur archer could have told him, *to
hit a target, one must aim above it.* When unable to
convince his Superior, it behooves the subordinate to
identify another executive, who preferably outranks his
Superior, and who unlike the latter happens to share the
subordinate's interest or point of view. Ideally, this is the
Superior's own supervisor. The subordinate passes his idea
on to this latter executive, in a packaging that suggests

---

* As the old Buddhist proverb says: "It is easy to convince an ignorant
man. It is even easier to convince a learned one. But the man who has
only the beginning of knowledge, Buddha himself cannot convince him!"

that there is something in it for him, and lets the man take over from there. Very soon the idea trickles down to the Superior, in the form of more or less coherent instructions and, coming from the right direction, it is promptly attended to and properly implemented. The method just described is also known under the trade name of "going over one's Superior's head," and is usually disliked by the Superior if he is aware of it, but when there is no other way of getting into the Superior's head, what else is there to do?* Just to make sure that the method is properly understood we shall also give a brief example of its application:

A former high-school basketball star was employed as expediter in the Purchasing Department of a Midwestern food processing and packaging plant located in his hometown. His times of glory on the local basketball courts were past, but his heart was still in the game, and he enjoyed few things more than occasionally coaching the youngsters of the town's high school basketball team. He had approached his supervisor at the plant for permission to take off one morning a week to work with the high-school kids, with the understanding that he would make up for time lost in overtime. But the boss, to his great chagrin, wouldn't hear of it. Then, one weekend in the spring, at a company-organized barbecue, he met the company's Vice-President in charge of Personnel and Public Relations. He explained to the Vice-President that

---

* A well-known variant of this method, that we note just for the record, is to send the Superior a memorandum, with carbon copies to those above him. To assure proper attention and general distribution, if the latter is felt necessary, the memorandum is marked "confidential"; "restricted" results in a slightly more limited circulation.

the local folks were making much of high-school basketball, and convinced him that helping the kids to improve
their play and win more games could do a great deal for
the company's image in the community (which, by the
way, could stand much improvement). The following
Monday, the Vice-President had a chat with the plant's
General Manager. The General Manager then called in
the head of the Purchasing Department and before the
day was out the immediate supervisor of our former
basketball star was only too glad to agree to release his
expediter for volunteer basketball coach duty two morn-
ings a week, on company time, and with no cut in pay.

The subordinate need not make any special efforts
to conceal, out of modesty or otherwise, the link between
his own thinking and that coming from above. Quite to
the contrary. Once this link has been gently but clearly
impressed in the mind of the Superior, the roundabout
transmittal of information will become, in fact, super-
fluous, and the subordinate can speak to his Superior with
the authority vested in top management itself.

## THE "QUOTING CHAIRMAN MAO" GAMBIT

A variation on the application of the principle described at the beginning of this chapter is the direct use
of wisdom emanating from above, or the "quoting Chairman Mao" gambit.

Every organization has its own resident Chairman
Mao, and a subordinate will find that a compendium of
the resident Chairman's pronouncements is a veritable
treasure trove of powerful and persuasive logic in any

management argument, irrespective of the side on which the subordinate may find himself (the Chairman is usually prolific, and has said something to suit every occasion). *Executives know that the Chairman is right, and waste no idle effort in questioning his opinions.* A ready quote from the Chairman's thought is an invaluable timesaving device for all concerned.

## THE USE OF THE SPOKEN WORD:
## AN ILLUSTRATION OF THE
## INFORMATION LEAK TECHNIQUE

Every so often, a subordinate is confronted with the intrepid "Feather Snatcher" type of Superior, bubbling with original ideas—none his own. In his frantic drive for recognition and promotion this "glory or bust, and credits (but mine) be damned" artist will claim for himself all and any achievements and ideas for improvements of his subordinates, even if they are in a strictly nonexecutive category (and to get the latter, he is not above burglarizing the employee suggestion box). He is like the banyan tree, under which nothing grows, and must be properly trimmed. This must be done swiftly and ruthlessly, for in the intensely competitive, insecure and compulsive executive world such examples may be catching, and antisocial phenomena of this nature, as weeds, must not be allowed to spread.

The scenario on how to deal with these cases of simpleminded and selfish executive ambition is straightforward, and is just one of the many examples of application of the Radović Rule. It is best illustrated by an actual incident, taken from the case file of an East Coast advertising agency:

The Account Executive responsible for the Media Advertising of the Foods Account was a supervisor of the type just described. No media man in the Media Advertising Department was ever given credit for suggesting improvements in food products and packaging; the Account Executive mentioned claimed to the Advertising Vice-President of the client food company, without blushing, that all such worthwhile ideas originating in the ad agency were his very own.

One day, a media man thought of a new and better way to repackage bean soup and other bean products for the growing health foods market, at a considerable increase in profit for the food processing company. He first found a pretext to contact the Advertising Vice-President of the client company, and as if in passing explained his idea to the latter. Saying nothing of this conversation, he then explained it again to his boss, the Account Executive. No sooner was this done than the Account Executive ran off to see the Advertising Vice-President of the client company, and claimed for himself credit for a new, valuable idea. Halfway through his story, the Advertising Vice-President interrupted him, completed the story himself, and added that this was an old idea of *his own,* that he never had the time to implement because of more pressing matters. He then curtly dismissed the crestfallen Account Executive, admonishing him to come next time with something more original.

After this trick was played on the Account Executive on several occasions, he became much more chary about

Every so often, a subordinate is confronted with the intrepid "Feather Snatcher" type of Superior, bubbling with original ideas—none of his own.

claiming as his own the efforts and achievements of others, to the satisfaction and amusement of media men.

## THE USES OF THE WRITTEN WORD

*The majority of executives have no fear of their own spoken word,* a perishable commodity that self-destructs after use and leaves no incriminating residue. Most of them also believe that they can talk their way in and out of and around anything, for that is what speech is for, after all. *But the written word is evidence,* and a Superior is not about to leave his calling card where it might not do him much good. It is helpful for the subordinate to keep a mental note of these executive idiosyncrasies, as the reader will presently see:

The supervisor of the Building Management and Maintenance Service at the headquarters of a large West Coast dry-goods merchandiser believed, rightly or wrongly, that doing special facors for the VIPs in the organization was the best way to protect his job and assure his future advancement with the company. He not only gladly accepted but actively solicited private no-charge odd jobs from the higher-ups, and the electricians, mechanics, carpenters and other craftsmen of the BM&MS were forever busy repairing radios, TVs, toasters, etc., or making bookshelves, cabinets and the like for the company's executives. For this work, for obvious reasons, the supervisor kept no official records, but gave only verbal orders.

The craftsmen in the BM&MS strongly objected to these dealings, not so much on moral grounds, as because the jobs meant more work for them and interfered with their own little private deals that they were using the BM&MS basement workshops for. However, they did not want an open showdown with their supervisor either, because an investigation of the matter would not only incriminate the supervisor, but would also show that they themselves were not altogether clean. So, of their own initiative, ostensibly for the sake of better records management, they started keeping a log on jobs for which no written work orders were issued by the supervisor, with detailed entries for time spent and materials used (all entries, incidentally, were also recorded on carbon copies, as insurance against the originals disappearing). Then they proudly showed to their supervisor their contribution to better management. The man, visualizing the internal auditors getting hold of the log, took sick for a week. But, on his return to work, special assignments for the benefit of the company brass came to an almost complete halt, giving the craftsmen of the BM&MS more leisure time to spend on their private projects (which, by the way, continued to go totally unrecorded).

*The examples given so far* in this chapter *are all variations* on the classical form *of the information leak technique, but information management is by no means confined to this.* The shuffling of file folders for instance, mentioned elsewhere, is a multipurpose device that should also be classified under the data management heading. Its use and effectiveness as such is well illustrated by the case history of Jerome Unterschlag, a sneaky, double-crossing and up-and-coming young executive in the Exploration Division of a large oil company. Jerome had a bright assistant whom he worked mercilessly, never acknowledg-

ing the assistant's efforts, and hogging for himself all the
credit for the assistant's work. Fed up, the assistant asked
for a transfer, but Jerome blocked it, and the assistant
then began thinking of some way to get Jerome himself
transferred, as an even better solution to his problem.
"Inadvertently," he filed the latest confidential information on activities by the competition in sheikhdom X,
indicating a fabulous oil potential, in the folder of sheikhdom Y, where the only mineral find ever made or likely
ever to be made is sand. Then he passed this folder to
Jerome for the meeting of the Executive Committee on
New Operations, which met quarterly to decide on opening up new oil fields. Jerome, a supersalesman (but rather
weak on delivery),* made a brilliant presentation, was
promoted right then and there to Manager of Sheikhdom
Y Operations, and dispatched forthwith to the field.

That was five years ago. Now and then, there is still
a word from Jerome. The latest news his family got was
through a recently returned Peace Corps volunteer. The
youngster, while still abroad a few months ago, got lost
in the desert while on a camel joyride. After three harrow-
ing days, he was rescued by the bedouins of Sheikh
Abdullah, the wise and amiable ruler of sheikhdom Y.
That is how he met Jerome Unterschlag. Jerome, the
youth reported, was trying very hard, over narghile, end-
less finjans of coffee, and an occasional sheep's eye, to
persuade Sheikh Abdullah to nationalize all foreign enterprises in his domain (so that he, Jerome, would have an

---

* A characteristic executive trait, developed in response to the correct
premise that even modest achievement takes time, but first-class promises
can be made on the spot.

excuse to pack and go home).\* But Abdullah was reluctant to do this, mainly for three reasons: First, Jerome is his only source of foreign exchange, and Jerome's continued residence in sheikhdom Y is indispensable for the favorable solution of the country's balance of payments problems; second, his presence in Abdullah's oasis is adding a sophisticated cosmopolitan flavor to the place; third, there are no other foreign enterprises in sheikhdom Y.

Rumors also form a variant of information but, because of their exceptional importance among the media of communication, rumors rate a separate chapter.

---

\* Jerome, incidentally, spoke broken Arabic, with a heavy accent and a lot of *chutzpah.*

**9**

# Rumors

> He ceas'd; but left so pleasing on the ear
> His voice, that list'ning still they seemed to hear.
>
> Homer: *Odyssey*

News never has the impact of rumors. News may never reach its intended destination, rumors always do. Rumor adds credibility to information that news can never match. Rumor can tell more in a sentence than news in a page. *Among information media, rumor has no peer.*

## A BASIC PRINCIPLE

The intrinsic value of rumors is, as a rule, well known to executives, and their intelligence radar is always on special alert for them. But *for rumors concerning a Superior to have full impact on him, he must be insecure.* When this condition is satisfied, rumors assure an inexhaustible supply of additional insecurity in a Superior. Properly conditioned by other applications of the Radović Rules, a Superior will always give a desired response to the rumor stimulus and, in the process, become still better attuned to management by subordinates. The conditioning itself may occasionally take a little time, and require patience on the part of the subordinate, because some executives have the staying power of a used aluminum can thrown away at the beach (but "little by little grow the bananas," as they say in Zaïre (Congo-Kinshasa, that is)).

## THE VERSATILITY OF THE MEDIUM

Depending on the circumstances, rumors can be made, added to, updated, modified, rerouted, etc. They can be aimed directly at the ultimate recipient, or in some other direction to have its effects bounced on to him. On occasion, they can be made *to serve a double purpose.* Namely, while concerning the alleged activities of one executive, *a rumor can be rumored as coming from another executive.* This double-duty play will contribute to the insecurity of both executives, and will in addition create useful tensions, frictions and suspicions among the executive confrerie.

## THE DOUBLE-PURPOSE RUMOR
## —A CASE HISTORY

A case history on the double-purpose rumor is not out of place at this point, and it takes us back to seventeenth-century France, to the times of Louis XIII, Richelieu, and the Three Musketeers:

Jules Saucisson was a lowly clerk attached to the office of that insufferable prig, the cross-eyed but financially clairvoyant Count Justin de Beauregard, Deputy Superintendent of Finances. The Count had on several occasions expressed himself disparagingly on Saucisson's professional talents, and Saucisson saw in the Count a serious threat to his ambitions (which, as appeared later, were anything but modest), that one way or the other had to be removed. Mischievously, Saucisson created a rumor to the effect that the boorish Duke Panteleymon Dourakhine, Envoy of the Czar of All Russias to the Court of France (Saucisson also had an anti-Russian bias), had said that Constance, Countess de Beauregard *
was readily available (which was true, common knowledge, and an innocuous remark), but not worth the effort (which was a lie, utterly devoid of courtly grace, and highly offensive). Ably fostered by Saucisson, the rumor

---

* Succintly described by a contemporary chronicler with the memorable vignette *qui ne l 'a pas vu, ne l 'a pas eu*—"who hasn't seen her, hasn't had her."

spread, and this left the Count de Beauregard no choice
but to lightly slap the Duke across the face with a heavy
perfumed glove, and the Duke, stuck with protocol, no
choice but to reluctantly challenge the Count to a duel
with pistols, although they both were confirmed cowards.
As neither of the two had the reputation of being a good
shot, Saucisson, who was told to help with the duel ar-
rangements, made sure that the pistols were loaded by
mistake with buckshot, to equitably improve the odds on
both sides. The duel went over without fatalities, but the
exterior of both contestants was rather badly punctured,
and they had to be retired from their respective Government Services, just as Saucisson had hoped.*

## FINISHING TOUCHES

*A touch of objectivity and compassion* in launching
or passing on a rumor *will add to* its *credibility* and
smooth its way, and at the same time establish the good

---

* The sequel to this case history is an instructive warning against executive aspirations in a subordinate: Saucisson, as it turned out, was an
executive postulant. By dint of clever scheming, he rose fast in the
Civil Service hierarchy, and in a few short years he was occupying the
post of Deputy Superintendent of Finances, previously held by his former
Superior, the Count de Beauregard. But then, promptly, he himself fell
victim to the same double-purpose rumor he had made such good use
of in the past. Saucisson, by now Viscount du Boudin, was goaded
against the notorious and much self-confessed womanizer Count Giovanni
Amatutte, the envoy of Naples, and had to challenge him to a duel. With
the assistance of chianti, Count Amatutte could shoot reasonably straight
even under conditions of great emotional stress, and therefore no buckshot precaution was taken on this occasion. And so Jules Saucission paid
the ultimate price for his foolish ambition.

*Anonymity and shadow play are the essence of a good rumor game.*

faith of the source. The body of the rumor, for instance, can be prefaced by a recounting of the qualities and past achievements of the executive in question, and distress can be expressed because of the facts brought out in the open by the rumor. Cases are known where such enlightened approach to rumor dissemination has even made a man feel good on account of his own sincere attempts at objectivity and fair play. There is a good deal to be said for the power of positive thinking.

## A WARNING AND A RECOMMENDATION

No matter how imaginative and elegant a rumor may be, the mature and wise subordinate will resist the temptation to claim credit for it. This not only will shield him from the persecution creative people are so often subjected to but, more importantly, will also add immeasurably to the effectiveness of the rumor. *Anonymity and shadow play are the essence of a good rumor game,* and restraint of pride and vanity in the originator of a rumor will always pay off in more impressive results.

Rumor is a most powerful and versatile management tool which, in the hands of an expert, brings the Radović Rule to life. *The subordinate is well advised to school himself early in the applications of this medium,* so that he can use it with efficiency and responsibility. Any effort made here pays many times over. A man recognized as an authority on the subject is in an enviable position of strength, and due respect is always shown to him. His relationship with his Superior and other executives will be a most satisfying and fruitful one, and he can with certainty look forward to a bright professional future (although, we admit, we do not expect everybody to show quite the same confidence in the future as the owners of the Chinese restaurant who listed in their menu the item "one-hundred-year-old eggs (aged on premises)").

**10**

# The woman executive

Despite my thirty years of research into the feminine soul,
I have not yet been able to answer . . . the great question
that has never been answered: What does a woman want?
Sigmund Freud

*Defies analysis. Best avoided.*

*I have not yet been able to answer . . . the great question that has never been answered: What does a woman want?*

# 11

# Building a reputation for hard work and competence

Many a bum show has been saved by the flag.
George M. Cohan

*An established reputation for hard work and competence very much strengthens the position of the subordinate vis-à-vis his Superior.* It is not only a shield, as is deodorant; it is an attack weapon, as is perfume. In the race for organizational supremacy it gives the subordinate a head start, and makes it difficult for the Superior ever to catch up with him. Even if the Superior does, if the reputation is widespread enough, there is no way for him

111

to get around it, and harass the subordinate as lazy or incompetent.

## THE REPUTATION FOR HARD WORK

The first thing to know is that *the reputation for hard work is not built on results, but on observable activity and visual displays.* To think otherwise is a cardinal mistake that can lead only to wasted time and effort and sure failure. As Madison Avenue well knows, the customer derives much more satisfaction in wearing a fancy label than the garment that comes with it. Similarly, with reputation, it is also the impression that counts, and not the substance.

A good illustration of what is meant by observable activity and visual displays is provided by our versatile old acquaintance, the office files. The periodic rearranging of files is a conspicuous and effective observable activity if it is done with *savoir-faire,* with papers well spread and overflowing onto adjoining desks and on the floor. The accent of the exercise, to be sure, is on spreading the papers, not arranging them. Office files also make eye-catching and very useful visual displays when manila folders are kept out of filing cabinets, prominently stacked on top of these, and bulging with telling evidence of one's hard work for everyone to see. Keeping in the folders extra copies of every document, or even unrelated printed matter makes them look impressively thick. The content of the folders does not really matter, especially if they are fitted with colored index tabs.

The *IN* and *OUT* desk paper trays give another ex-

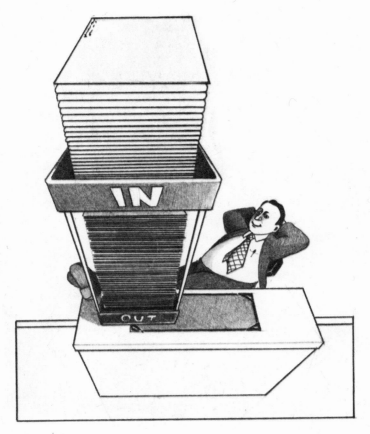

*The subordinate's* IN *and* OUT *desk paper trays play an important role in conveying the amount of work he turns out.*

ample of the effective use of visual displays. Although many subordinates may not be aware of this, these trays do play an important role in conveying an idea of the amount of work they turn out. There are two different schools of thought on whether to keep the *IN* tray full or empty. An empty *IN* tray may convey an impression of efficiency, but may also be interpreted as an indication of no work being done. A full *IN* tray is similarly subject to two different interpretations, one of a flood of work coming in, and the other of inefficiency. The drawbacks of both approaches can be avoided by bringing the *OUT* tray into the picture: The *IN* tray is kept empty but the *OUT* tray is kept full, with strict instructions to the secretary to leave it that way (the occasional papers she is supposed to file or type are put somewhere else). This solution combines the two effects of high output and efficiency and gives, as a bonus, the additional impression that the secretary just can't keep up with her hardworking boss. As a precaution, however, display material in the *OUT* tray should occasionally be replaced with one of different shape and color.

*In building up a reputation for hard work,* as in other matters, the useful details should not be overlooked, for as everybody knows *it is often the small things that really count* (and, incidentally, that is why small debts should always be paid back). A good deal of mileage can be obtained out of their cumulative effect. For instance: Sandwiches for lunch should not be carried in a brown paper bag, but in a briefcase, to look like homework; a haggard appearance in the morning should be related to heavy work load, and not attributed to a rough night out; a summons to a business meeting should always be countered first by "checking the calendar" and then a request to change the time because of conflicting "earlier commitments" on the work agenda for the day. Some people, mindful of their reputation, will even go as far as to come early to the office and leave late,* usually to read newspapers undisturbed. (Trouble is, with work ethics these days in alarming decline, there is seldom anyone around to witness the long hours the subordinate puts in and corroborate his dedication to work. Moreover, this time-consuming practice may also give the Superiors the preposterous notion that they can expect overtime from the subordinates as a matter of course, and it therefore must be labeled as second-rate tactics.)

## THE REPUTATION FOR COMPETENCE

For reasons given in Chapter II of this Guide, the subordinate has already been advised to seek positions that arouse little interest in Superiors and other subordinates. Among other things, an employee holding a supposedly dull and unpopular job will seldom be asked to prove his real or claimed qualifications for it. But, by the same token, he will find it difficult to show his ex-

---

* While the tactical merit of leaving the office late is certainly overrated, there is no harm in leaving early, provided this is done sensibly: Proper early-leaving time is at least three-quarters of one hour to one hour before others, and not an obvious and useless five or ten minutes before quitting time. Before leaving, instructions are left with the secretary to inform all callers that one has "just stepped out of the office and is somewhere in the building." The chances, incidentally, of remaining undetected "somewhere in the building," even if not there, are much better in a large concern, and this opportunity for privacy is another advantage of working for an organization of some size.

pertise to others, if he wishes to do so in order to better entrench himself in his job or out of professional vanity. The sad truth is that *to demonstrate his professional competence to anyone, the subordinate often needs a captive audience.*

While there is no denying that a subordinate may not be able to round up at will a suitable captive audience, the problem he faces is really less serious that it at first appears. Opportunities are always there, and a wide-awake subordinate, such as our friend Harry Pelican, the quality control inspector in a shoe factory, will easily recognize them. Several years ago, at the time Mr. Hornbill was still giving him much trouble, Harry figured that if he only could demonstrate to Mr. van Loon his thorough knowledge of the principles of statistical quality control, Hornbill would have an awfully hard time getting him fired, if he ever decided to try that. So for several days he exerted himself to commit to memory a few pages of a manual on statistical quality control, and also observed Mr. van Loon's habits and movements. And then he cornered Mr. van Loon in the men's room, under circumstances which allowed the latter no easy escape:

"Good morning, Mr. van Loon. I can tell you by your shiny shoes," said Harry, installing himself in a cubicle of the men's room next to the one already occupied by Mr. van Loon. "How are you today?"

"I am fine Harry, thank you." came Mr. van Loon's reply from the other side of the three-quarter-length partition, followed by a cautious "So far."

"As I was beginning to explain to you, sir, the day before yesterday, just before you remembered you had to run off to a meeting, the Average Outgoing Quality Limit

Double Sampling Plan is a natural for our operation. Its whole concept for controlling quality is based. . . ."

"Harry, do you always mix business and pleasure?" inquired Mr. van Loon plaintively.

"The AOQL Double Sampling Plan is all pleasure, sir. Its whole concept is based on the 'go-no go' examination of a specific number of articles taken at random from a large group. You follow me, sir?"

"Sure, I follow you Harry. With my pants down, do I have any other choice?"

"The acceptance or rejection is normally made on the basis of results obtained from the first sample alone. However . . ."

"I'll take your word for it Harry, believe me."

"And the sampling working tables are already all made out. I just happen to have one with me, for the AOQL of 1.5 percent. Now. . . ."

"Harry, you are trying to convert a believer."

"Now just have a look for yourself." Harry pressed on, passing the table to van Loon under the partition. "Take any lot, there at the left, for a Process Average percent of, say, .03 to .04. . . ."

"For Pete's sake, Harry . . . you got me all confused. . . . I just flushed the table instead of. . . . Dammit!"

"That's all right, sir, no harm done. I have extra copies on my desk. I'll go get them right away. You just sit tight right where you are. I won't be a minute. . . ."

After this men's room conversation Harry's professional reputation was firmly established with van Loon, and there was very little Hornbill could do to undercut him on grounds of professional incompetence.

## SOME CAVEATS

In addition to advice on positive action aimed at building a reputation for hard work and competence, the reader should also be given a warning on some related don'ts.

For instance, *the speciously nonchalant approach to one's duties at work falls within the Superior's repertory of ploys, and has no place among the techniques of the Radović Rule.* Some executives use it to give proof of a rare competence and of an ability to deal effortlessly with all management problems (and usually fool no one but themselves), but this certainly is not the impression the subordinate wants to convey of himself. Such impression might make his job appear desirable and create competition for it or, worse, suggest that he is of executive caliber and promotable. *The impression the subordinate wants to make is one of competence arduously acquired and laboriously exercised.*

*Belittling the performance of one's fellow workers to make one's own look better by comparison is also a device that rightly belongs in the Superior's bag of tricks* (but this being an all-to-human foible, it often deserves our forgiveness \*). *Its usefulness for the subordinate is minimal;* in fact, it may even be harmful in that it creates unnecessary and negative tensions and frictions on the job. The difference can be easily explained by the law of supply and demand: Competition for executive positions is fierce. All candidates being uniformly outstanding

---

\* Fogiveness: a quality of heart that reconciles one man to the wrongs done to another.

(in expectations, if not ability), even the smallest advantage over another competitor counts. In such circumstances, naturally, a constructive and carefully circulated criticism of a competitor's shortcomings is most useful. But, for subordinate jobs, there is no ruthless competition. They can be gotten for the asking, and often go begging for the lack of demand. This being the case, preventive criticism of the kind just described amounts to no more than shadowboxing, and is often only an expression of innate wickedness. The subordinate can even praise fellow workers with impunity. This practice helps build a fine subordinate *esprit de corps,* and occasionally even creates a pleasant feeling of moral superiority in the subordinate, at no extra cost to him.

# 12

# Individual versus
# group actions

If you want to get rich, you son of a bitch,
    I'll tell you what to do:
Never sit down with a tear or a frown,
    And paddle your own canoe.

Anonymous

In this age of pervasive collectivism and throttled individualism, it is not astonishing that, with increasing frequency, Superiors and subordinates alike should band together, in two separate and opposing groups, to sort out some unsortable and thus ever-present problems of Superior-subordinate relationships. A whole slew of new, impersonal, machine-age-flavored, unpleasant-sounding words—collective bargaining, group actions, joint activ-

ities, team achievements, mass movements, popular participation, etc.—has appeared to mark this trend, and their
uninspired look is more than matched by their uninspiring
substance. But the trouble runs deeper than philology.

## UNITED WE STAND?

Of particular relevance to this chapter is what is
described as collective bargaining. Its function is presumably to improve the lot of the rank and file subordinate
by substituting group for individual undertakings, on the
assumption that two pounds per two square feet carry
more weight than one pound per one square foot, and
that by definition a chorus sounds better than a solo
singer.

The results and, worse, the ritual of collective bargaining are drearily insipid and predictable: Always the
same opening statements, to the word, with the same
modest and realistic demands, and the same magnanimous
and realistic counteroffers; same threats and counter-
threats, accompanied by the same histrionics; even the
faces become the same. Never a victory or a defeat, but
always a standoff. The routine of collective bargaining, to
put it charitably, is as imaginative and full of surprises
as that of an economy house of ill repute, only minus
the fun.

To boot, collective bargaining is a misleading mis-
nomer. *In collective bargaining, the opportunities for
meaningful participation by the subordinate and for the
expression of his creative instincts and capabilities are
next to nil.* His role is reduced to that assigned to him

In this age of pervasive collectivism and throttled individual-ism, it is not surprising that Superiors and subordinates should band together in two separate and opposing groups.

by his representatives, whether he shows talent and disposition for it or not: onlooker, picketer, slogan shouter, placard sandwich-man, resolution signer, opposition baiter, brick thrower, sidewalk pugilist and the like. No room is left for individual initiative and contribution. The fulfilling excitement of the face-to-face, *corrida*-like situation where man survives and wins by his own wits is sadly lacking. Even the representatives of the subordinates are not representative at all of what the subordinate is. They are really Superiors masquerading in subordinate garb, only they are more demanding, more arrogant and hypocritical, and more troublesome to deal with than the genuine breed. The subordinate needs them like he needs a mother-in-law.

Even a casual analysis unmistakably reveals that *collective action is at best of marginal utility to a capable subordinate, and* that *it can play only a minor supporting role next to individual action.* The latter alone can provide complete-package, tailor-made solutions to a subordinate's career plans, and reap for him the abundant rewards of which our Rule speaks. A subordinate who relies entirely on collective action to take care of his occupational problems and aspirations is no smarter than the man who believes he can court and win a girl by proxy, and no more successful. He is also robbing himself of many fruitful, creative and deeply satisfying years of individualized subordinate insubordination.

The role of collective action in the shaping of their respective careers also brings out one of the basic differences between the Superior and the subordinate: What the Superior (or executive aspirant for that matter) dreams about—to climb up the executive ladder—he cannot do by himself. He knows this and acknowledges it by joining fraternities and clubs, by insinuating himself into coteries and cliques, by observing brotherhood discipline and paying homage to gang elders, by participating in mob vendettas and tong wars, etc. In more than one way, he willingly pays his union dues. But *that which the subordinate wants—independence from others—he can by definition only achieve by himself.* In fact, alone he stands, united he falls.

## A CASE HISTORY

Patrick Polenta, whose capsule case history we shall now give, found the truth of all this through hard experience. As a young man, Pat was an ardent believer in collective movements, and a frontline militant of labor-management disputes. For his troubles he often got the sack, and collected over the period of three prodigal years a total of twenty-three stitches in the scalp, four missing front teeth, $450 in fines, and seventy-five days in jail.* While cooling down in solitary, Pat had the time to reflect on the merits of collective action and on all the good it did him personally. Maybe, it occured to him, shifting for oneself rather than stepping strictly to the collective beat wasn't such a bad idea, after all.

Once out of jail he found himself a job as a power

---

* "But, Judge, that's too much! I was fighting for the rights of the masses," Pat protested his last sentence of thirty days in jail.

"The defendant obviously has the taste for wholesale," replied the judge "but this court, as it happens, dispenses justice at retail, and the prices are of necessity somewhat higher."

plant maintenance mechanic in a large steel mill—a job that usually did not require much more than his presence —and in his free time started picking up customers for his father-in-law's secondhand car business. Today, five years after he gave up on collective efforts to improve the world and instead devoted himself to the more modest task of bettering himself on his own, Pat is a silent (but very active and very prosperous) partner in the largest new car dealership in town, has a full-time job that does not interfere with, but nicely complements his business, enjoys both the respect of the management (as a successful businessman in his own right and a good man to know when a new car is needed) and the envy of the rank and file (a genuine recognition of success) and has the satisfaction of having achieved the lot all by himself.

# 13

# The use of secretarial assistance

Thou shalt not muzzle the mouth of the ox that treadeth out the corn.

*New Testament: 1 Cor. 9:9.*

While today it is generally acknowledged that woman has a place in society, her potential to make an invaluable contribution as office secretary goes sometimes unrecognized. The advantages of secretarial assistance are varied and many, but are very much reduced if a secretary is tied to a secretarial typing pool, which is as conducive to the flourishing of talent in the office as the assembly line is in the factory. *The secretary must be liberated*

127

*from the typing pool, to prevent her many gifts and ca-
pabilities from going to waste.* A subordinate should make
every effort possible to win his own personal secretary,
not as a questionable badge of success, but because of the
contribution she can make in this capacity to the subordinate cause. In the scence of Management of Superiors, it
is always well to remember, *the role of the secretary is not
decorative but strictly functional.* At least till 5 P.M. After
5 P.M., she is no longer a secretary, and the rules of a
different game apply. That game is beyond the scope of
this book.

## A PARTNERSHIP

*The relationship between a subordinate and his secre-
tary should be one of partnership.* Only by working in
harmony as a team can they really make the Radović
Rule work fully for them, and against their natural and
common opponent in the organization—the executive. But
even in a partnership someone must take the lead, and
that must be whoever has best mastered the Management
of Superiors. As things stand today, this is usually the
subordinate. But on occasion, a subordinate is either not
willing or not capable to assume leadership. His secretary
will then, whether she cares for it or not, have to guide
him, and he fully deserves it.

A subordinate and his secretary are so much of a
natural team that whatever one does will inevitably reflect on the other. If a secretary, for instance, is idle much
of the time it will generally be assumed that the subordinate she works with doesn't do much either. The

opposite is equally true, and *if his secretary looks like she is working hard and is prominently seated for all to notice, the subordinate she works with need hardly work at all.* Again, as in the case of the subordinate himself, she need not be actually working; *results of her work are unimportant, and it is visible activity that counts.* To entrust her, for example, with the periodic random reshuffling of files, already mentioned in an earlier chapter, will perfectly serve the purpose of creating the effect of bustle desired, especially if she has a disorganized mind and easily messes things up.

To work well in tandem is not always easy, particularly when people are selfish or have lapses of judgment. For instance, a subordinate will sometimes, mostly in the neophyte stages of his career when he knows no better, feel in himself a tinge of a desire to achieve executive rank. By the simple device of ordering his secretary around, he can savor the taste of executive status and, if he has the makings of a genuine subordinate, in the process get over this silly delusion of his. His secretary, however, is at the same time advised not to be all that understanding or patient, to show flight when pushed and even throw a temper tantrum if needed. This is guaranteed to make the subordinate's cure even more complete and rapid, to the benefit of both of them.

These and like spats and tiffs cannot always be avoided, but if one will just occasionally remember that *the secretary is* in fact *as much of a subordinate as the subordinate himself,* and that the Radović Rule is therefore meant for the benefit of both, there should be no basic difficulties between them that a little goodwill cannot overcome.

## SELECTING A SECRETARY

*If a choice is to be made, and a young, attractive secretary with a sweet disposition is pitted against a not-so-young and crotchety one with looks to match, the latter* wins hands down, and *must be given preference in hiring.* But let us explain this seemingly unorthodox selection:

Aware of her assets, the young one can become quite independent, even unreliable. She will have too many things on her mind, and will be unpredictable. She will generate too much traffic, which is bad for the privacy of the subordinate she works with. She may even get his attention for the wrong reasons, which have nothing to do with the management of his Superiors. Not being mature, she often does not have sense enough to distinguish the possible from the impossible, the advisable from that which is not. She can be of little use and much trouble to her teammate.

But the weathered one, she has strength of character, and she knows it. She is the veteran of many office battles, and has been losing few lately. She is ready and game to take on any comer, no matter what his corporate station. Her Cerberus-like presence at the side of the man she works with assures him all the tranquillity and peace necessary to pursue undisturbed the high road of subordinate life. It is true, all her quills are not pointing in the most desirable direction, and he is often painfully reminded of this. But, nothing is perfect in this world. She is also a fount of and a glutton for relevant information, and she is a pro on how to use it. Her advice is well worth listening to. She plays her part in the management games

If a choice is to be made, a not-so-young and crotchety secretary with looks to match, must be given the preference in hiring.

with consummate skill, and when interested enough, she plays it with vengeance, just for the sheer pleasure of it. She is good to have on one's side, and her allegiance can be earned and maintained with a smile in the morning, a flower for Valentine's Day and a sympathetic ear now and then. But pretense will not do. She has no illusions left, and knows sham when she sees or hears it. She may not be much to look at, or an unalloyed joy to listen to, but she makes worthwhile all the rigors of office life together.

## A TYPE TO CAREFULLY AVOID

Some secretaries are less cooperative than others, but with goodwill and patience they can be won over. *The real menace is the well-meaning-bumbler-cum-initiative type,* an unmitigated disaster for whomever she works with or for. It is difficult to explain to someone who hasn't experienced her how much frustration, anguish and damage she can cause, but the fact remains that, whether she works for an executive or is teamed with a subordinate, her good intentions pave either man's separate road to hell. And there isn't much one can do with or to her: One could try to train her and reform her, but this is a futile effort. Or one could shoot her or poison her, neither of which is very practical. The best the subordinate she works with can hope for is that if he tirelessly advertises her as a secretarial prodigy she may someday be snatched away from him and placed, like a time bomb, behind the typewriter in some executive suite. But if she is, on top of everything else, also loyal to him and does not want to leave him, he might as well resign and quit, because he is a doomed man.

## A CASE HISTORY

To end this chapter, a case history illustrating both the benefits and the perils of secretarial assistance will not be amiss: Barney Mimeo was a nice, clean-cut happy-go-lucky young man employed as junior internal auditor by a manufacturer of Venetian blinds. His secretary, whom he shared with another colleague, was dyspeptic, thin-lipped, fortyish Miss Prudence Espina, invariably dressed in classical Salvation Army chic, and intense as a Doberman pinscher. Redoubtable Miss Espina, whose tongue was generating even more acid than her stomach, was, for reasons of her own, very fond of Barney's care-free manner, and she provided him, free, with office protection of a quality that the Mafia could never aspire to sell.

But, one day, Miss Espina's stomach ulcers started acting up pretty badly, and she had to take an extended sick leave to undertake medical treatment and recuperate. Her temporary replacement was nineteen-year-old Clementine, easy on the eye and a fringe benefit to watch undulating down the corridor. Barney had a good look, too. What he saw, he liked, and he smiled; she responded; he proposed; she accepted; in that order. But she had mink on her mind, not just love and companionship. In search of the golden fleece, Barney applied for and got a supervisory job with a distributor of detergents. But he didn't have the makings of an executive and soon got fired. This touched the permafrost of Clementine's warm heart; she sued Barney for divorce and for alimony, and she goth both.

Barney is at his old desk now, counting the Venetian blinds, with Miss Espina keeping troubles at bay. A measure of serenity has been restored in his life, but the old *joie de vivre* is gone out of him. He has paid for not following the precepts of the Radović Rule.

We hope that his sad story will serve as a warning to the subordinate not to confuse the issues in the office, and to look to his secretary for help in managing his Superiors and not as a source of romance.

# 14

# The underprivileged label

Oh, I am in love with the janitor's boy.
Nathalia Crane: *The Janitor's Boy*

These are, without doubt, the times of the oppressed minority. To be, nowadays, part of the ruling majority is a clear handicap. Membership in a majority is an open invitation to vituperation, insults, vilification, denigration and other assorted forms of ill-treatment and abuse. One with the misfortune of belonging to a ruling majority pays levies to atone for his past sins and those of his father and relations, and earns nothing but contempt. He spends his time hiding in shame, dodging brickbats, or being lectured to. He has no friend in this world. The only place where he may rate personal attention is the Internal Revenue Service.

But to be in a wronged minority is altogether different. A man so fortunate will ask for what is his (or what he says is his), and it will be given to him. He will talk, and will be applauded. He will trespass, and a scientific study will be made of it. He will command respect and admiration, for he can say or do no wrong. Whatever his endeavors, they will be noble, selfless, normal, human, or at least socially redeeming.* And his friendships will be an embarrassment of riches. No subordinate can really afford to be without an underprivileged label.

## UNDERPRIVILEGE AND THE SUBORDINATE

A discerning subordinate will not procrastinate to establish *credentials in* at least a couple of *underprivileged groups*. This *will immeasurably strengthen the subordinate's offensive and defensive posture vis-à-vis his Superior.* No executive in his right mind will risk being accused of discrimination and bias against, say, a Fellow of the Flat Earth Society, a believer in the Contemplation of the Navel (who steadfastly practices on the job), or the last of the Tasmanians. He knows better than to arouse the wrath of those with an exquisite sense of social justice and fair play, and open himself wide to attacks as oppressor or exploiter of the underdog. But he

---

* He is, in a way, like the American chicken, which lays "medium," "large," "extra-large" and "jumbo" eggs, but never "small" ones.

will often be found queueing up, with the rest of the management, and all the way round the block, to pay homage and make a sincere offer of his disinterested services to the underprivileged, so as to establish his own credentials as their friend in good standing. This also makes a very good label, considered in management circles well worth a bit of voluntary and potentially rewarding masochism. Or, to say it in somewhat more lay terms, many a Superior does not really mind having his behind kicked in if this just might propel him a little forward in executive rankings. (In all fairness, it should also be explained immediately that all this, and much more, is typically done only for the good of the organization. It makes one sometimes wonder, though, why, with so many selfless and dedicated executives around, always ready to put the interests of the organization before their own, the average organization is not doing any better.)

## SELECTING THE UNDERPRIVILEGED LABEL

There are status strata as well among those claiming they are discriminated against, and *the subordinate should not bother joining any but the very elite of the underprivileged.* This elite is identified in the same way the best rock music is, by its score on the decibel scale.* But, as with musical tastes, fashion affects underprivileged rankings as well, and the alert subordinate will always

---

* An eminent psychologist actually maintains that most of the contemporary music is pure noise, designed to block out any thinking process in the listener. And there, he adds, is also the explanation for its great popular appeal.

keep track of any such shifts, and nimbly keep his affiliations up to date.

How important it is to be in the right group at the right time and place the reader can judge for himself from the account of the following incident which took place in Chicago one cold windy night in late November 1956:

Two Russian exchange students at the University of Chicago, their fur caps folded over their ears, were trudging their way to their dormitory after a long, dreary evening in the stacks of the main campus library. As they were approaching International House, where they both were residents, they were jumped by four hoodlums and relieved at knifepoint of their wallets. As the wallet transfer transaction was taking place, the two students were muttering to themselves in Russian something like, "This is capitalism for you!" and, "This is no peaceful co-existence." Hearing words he could not understand, the top hood inquired:

"You guys not Americans?"

"No, we are not Americans," replied the two Russians in unison, "we are Russian exchange students."

"Well, why the hell don't you say so!" exclaimed the hoodlum, folding his switchblade shut with a flourish and handing the billfolds back to the Russians. "Here are your wallets! We don't want you to get the wrong impression of this country!"

It is doubtful that today, more than fifteen years later, it would very much help in a similar situation to be a Russian exchange student. Maybe mainland Chinese.

*The subordinate need not actually join any group to reap the advantages of underprivilege. A claim will usually suffice,* as membership will seldom be checked upon. Even if a check is made, findings cannot be used, for this would only prove management's persecution tactics. Joining often complicates matters and takes valuable time that is better used for other purposes, not to speak of the burden of tiresome and silly obligations it may impose. If one can think of a catchy name that unmistakably rings of an accredited kind of deprivation or discrimination or both, any real underprivileged group can be dispensed with. This may in fact well be the most effective and most comfortable way of wearing the underprivileged label. It works like instant bottle-suntan, only better.

## A CASE HISTORY

That to be underprivileged makes good employment sense is clearly demonstrated by the case history of Jonah Gooseberry, junior accountant of long standing for an appliances manufacturer in the Greater New York area. Jonah claimed to be the scion of a long line of destitute migrant cherry-picking farm laborers. His family, he often used to recall with emotion welling up in his voice, had to make great sacrifices to give him an education. Unlike other cherry pickers, who worked the regular June–July season, his family, to support him through school, had to start picking cherries in early April, and often would go on picking them well into November. Jonah felt a deep sense of indebtedness to his cherry-picking family and had firmly resolved, while still in school, to devote himself to the betterment of the cherry pickers' lot. He was, he often boasted, a founding member and a Vice President

of the United Cherry Pickers' League, but had to hold
another paying job as the League was too poor to pay
its officers. Jonah's social conscience, selflessness and dedication to the cherry pickers' cause was not lost on his
employer, and there never were any objections to his
frequent absences from work on League business, which
he usually transacted at the Long Island "Big A" racetrack.


## ANOTHER CAVEAT

Before going on to the next chapter, just one short
warning would seem to be called for: The subordinate
should not be so naive as to assume that the possibilities
of the underdog gambit have no limits and can be extended to include a straight plea for fair play. Human
magnanimity has natural bounds, and preposterous demands on it should not be made. A subordinate who
shows no consideration for this and cries foul will justly
be branded as an impertinent fool, and any executive
worth half his salt will know how to take care of this
troublemaker in short order. *The subordinate who invokes
and expects fair play is fair game for his Superior.*

*He was a founding member and a Vice President of the*
*United Cherry Pickers' League . . .*

**15**

# The subordinate image

A man should never put on his best trousers when he goes
out to battle for freedom and truth.

Ibsen: *An Enemy of the People*

Although he may be able to coax incomparable sounds
out of the orchestra with his baton, a conductor will never
win public acclaim as a great artist unless he can at the
same time give a visually satisfying dance performance on
top of his little stand. Similarly, *even the best qualified
subordinate will not go very far unless he has a good
image with which to back up his substance. Often, an
adequate image is all he needs to get by nicely.*

A good image is a work of art and, as a work of art, depends on illusion for its effect on the beholder. But one need not be a gifted artist to create a good subordinate image; faithfully following the instructions of the paint-by-number amateur painting kit is all that is required.

## THE ELEMENTS OF A GOOD SUBORDINATE IMAGE

*The most important impression the subordinate image should convey is one of independence of spirit,* an independence it is no use trying to break down. It is a grave mistake, however, to believe that a satisfactory impression of an indomitable spirit can be achieved by sporting locks of unruly long hair and other defiant hair growth, by wearing colored love-bead necklaces, sleeveless shirts and gaily striped bell-bottom pants cut low on the hip, or by boldly staring the executives down. Nothing could be more erroneous. *A rebellious public attitude betrays a lack of inner conviction and of self-assurance and, even worse, often awakens in Superiors that perverse Samaritan impulse to help and save an erring soul* (which can make a fiery rebel feel as if his solemn challenge has been answered by a solicitous and sincere offer of a pacifier, and drive him plumb crazy). Moreover, extravagant behavior is easily subject to misinterpretation, as in the case of the young man who burned incense in his office as a sign of protest against his company's lack of ecological conscience, and was classified in Personnel's confidential files as "a deeply religious

*The impression of an indomitable spirit cannot be achieved by sporting locks of unruly long hair or wearing colored love bead necklaces, sleeveless shirts, and gaily striped bell-bottom pants.*

person" (which, objectively speaking, was not necessarily bad for him, but certainly was not the image he wanted to project, and would have vexed him to no end had he known).

The correct impression to give is one of simple, natural and effortless raw strength of character, plainly and hopelessly beyond redemption. A close crew-cut appearance will be just fine. Functional clothing, strictly designed to protect against the weather and looking it, will also help. So will placidly chewing gum at meetings. The proper behavior in the unlikely event of being invited to lunch by a Superior is to concentrate on food and waste no time on useless conversation, insist on Rheingold beer if offered French wine, and ask the waiter for second and third helpings. A tabloid sticking out of the hind pocket folded at the parimutuel data page will nicely round out the desired picture. Confronted with our man, even the most resolute and hardened Superior will feel helpless and will give up even the idea of trying to convince, manipulate or use him, as the case may be.

## A NOTE OF CAUTION

But the subordinate should not become enamored of his own image, or begin to cherish his status symbols for their own sake rather than valuing them only as means to an end. If he does, he will soon find himself in pretty much the same predicament as the all-too-common executive who goes to the VIP john to reassure himself of his personal stature and worth, and not for a more satisfying if more prosaic reason, who does not look out of his window to watch the pretty girls pass by, but to count the number of glass panels his rank entitles him to, and who does not stand on his own two feet, but on his office carpet.

## AN ILLUSTRATION

There are many ways to build an effective subordinate image, and the case history of Joe Pomidoro, warehouse inventory clerk for a large distributor of automotive parts, only suggests the range of possibilities.

Joe Pomidoro built his entire image, and with it his entire career, on the smell of garlic. Joe loved garlic, without qualification and reservation, and could not keep away from it despite the heavy social toll it made him pay. But one day, as Joe was reflecting on his lot in odoriferous solitude, it occured to him that garlic plays no favorites. It kept at a distance pretty girls, but it kept at a respectful distance his supervisor as well. From this point on, Joe made every working day a garlic day. His boss, who could think of no smell fouler than garlic's, atempted to outsmart him by giving him orders over the phone, but Joe developed poor hearing and would come running to his boss for instructions at close range. The boss then tried memoranda, but Joe was always in need of verbal explanations. In desperation, the boss turned to Personnel, with a plea to intercede and try to change Joe's dietary habits. But Personnel, on the grounds that such intervention would represent an overt act of discrimination against a member of a minority where garlic is part of the national heritage, flatly refused to intervene. The boss caved in, and had a desk for Joe set up in a remote corner of the warehouse, with a virtual carte blanche for him to do whatever he wanted as long as it involved no contact between the two of them. This was pretty much what Joe was after, for his goals in life were modest enough: A weekly paycheck without too much strain, uninterrupted siestas after lunch and time enough for building sailing-ship models in bottles—which was his very favorite pastime. And thus, we note in passing, yet another item was added, in the field of personnel management, to the already impressive list of proven advantages to be derived from regularly eating garlic.

# 16

# The subordinate ethics

Some people wanted champagne and caviar when they should have had beer and hot dogs.
Dwight D. Eisenhower: *Speech,* St. Andrews Society, 1949

Without a clear idea of what is good for him, a person will find himself, in his ignorance, listening at street corners to the rhetoric of assorted kooks, obscurantists, blabbering half-wits and raving maniacs and, which is even more disturbing, will be taking them seriously. To realize that this is not an exaggeration, but rather a wide-spread symptom of a general malaise—the confusion of the times we live in—one need only switch the TV or radio on, open a newspaper or attend a live rally or demonstration and see for oneself how ready, rapt and enthusiastic an audience any nonsense and drivel can find these days.

A subordinate without clear guidelines for organizational behavior similarly faces the danger of getting lost in the corporate maze, and falls easy victim to executive blandishments, threats and obfuscations. Simple awareness of the Radović Rule, the truth and value of which we hope are by now firmly established in the reader's mind, will by itself give the subordinate confidence and a firm footing in his dealings with Superiors, but a functional code of conduct, both to protect him and to tell him what positive action any situation calls for is also needed. However, for such a code to work, the subordinate must cling to it with tenacity, and must not ride his convictions sidesaddle fashion, ready to slide off them at first signs of discomfort.

The space available does not allow for a detailed listing and explanation of all the do's and don'ts of subordinate behavior, but neither is this necessary: Decisions the subordinate has to make are basically moral decisions, and he really need only consult his own conscience to tell him what to do and what not to. Consequently, for all practical purposes, all that is required is a simple and short moral reminder, a handy code of ethics or subordinate credo in the shape of, say, the subordinate Ten Commandments. It could read something like this:

By Woolworth's, the Mets, Coney Island and Hubert Humphrey, and other such temples and champions of the Common Man (May his shadow never grow shorter!),

*The subordinate Ten Commandments.*

I solemnly swear always to observe and uphold the following:

I shall not gape in envy at the empty promises up the management ladder, nor spend my days straining my back to reach the plastic carrot at the end of the executive incentive stick.

I shall, instead, acquire humble and even despised subordinate skills and—a corporate pariah—become untouchable (and indispensable).

I shall not be ashamed of my subordinate status but, knowing that I am irreplaceable, shall flaunt my modest qualifications (be they real or presumed) and exact from management due respect, recognition and privileges.

I shall become a diligent student of company rules and regulations, and through constant practice on my Superior, shall learn how to use this wonderful management tool to keep him on a course that is both safe for him and beneficial for me.

I shall choose my acquaintances not only for pleasure but, being aware of the phenomenon of guilt or credit by association, for demonstration value as well. And if my social contacts seem somewhat deficient, I shall get the benefit of the doubt for those I just might have.

I shall loyally warn my Superior of all threats (be they real, possible, probable or improbable) to his position and ambitions, and ensure that he never relaxes his guard against his fellow executives. Recognizing that supervision of my work hinders him in this endeavor, I shall helpfully relieve him of that responsibility and assume it myself.

I shall generously administer recognition and respect to my Superior, knowing that softened clay is easier to mold. Occasionally, I shall also give him a public accolade he will at least remember if not gratefully cherish me for.

I shall not gather intelligence for the sake of idle curiosity, nor shall I hoard it if I can pass it on to good effect. And where necessary information is scarce or ill-fitting I shall create it, tailor-made to fill the existing need.

I shall not underestimate my secretary, nor frivolously treat her as a plaything, but will recognize in her a fellow subordinate, and work with her in a true spirit of teamwork. But the woman executive, whose purpose in this world remains a mystery, I shall resolutely avoid.

I shall not give in to the herd instinct and substitute collective will and wisdom for my own because, just as the race is to the swift and the battle, maybe, to the brave, God surely helps him best who helps himself.

I shall not be ashamed of my underprivileged antecedents, but will wear them proudly on my lapel, even if I have to borrow them, for the kingdom of the informed humble and poor is here, complete with status and fringe benefits.

I shall cultivate a functional subordinate image designed, not unlike the rattle at the end of the rattler's tail, to give clear warning to my Superior, thus avoiding the waste of his time and mine in a confrontation with a foregone conclusion.

And may the Superior's lot afflict me (as it surely will) if I disregard these Commandments.

# Epilogue

No book, to tell the truth, can do more for its reader than a baedeker: It can show him the way, but it cannot pay his fare. We hope, however, that this little volume has made the destination appear attractive enough and the journey sufficiently exciting to induce the subordinate who reads it to embark, on his own, on a trip he can well afford: From a world where the Superior has him over the barrel to a world where it is more the other way around.